FINDING THE WAY

Searching for the Roots of Christianity

Jerry Ford

DEDICATION

To the memory of the Reverend K. Barry Passmore, a dedicated minister who always found the time to encourage an inquisitive teenager.

"Seek and you will find, knock and the door will be opened; everything that is hidden will be revealed to you."

Jesus the Nazarene

"God has placed us on many different roads, but we are all seeking the same destination."

George Code (c.1920), Rural Dean, Ontario Diocese, Anglican Church of Canada

Table of Contents

Author's Preface

I was born into a family where Christian values were the subtext of our lives. We lived our faith, there was not much need for discussion and analysis because we were raised to always do the right thing. We instinctively knew what that was because it was the way we lived, the way our parents led us by example through their own lives of service. A lifelong commitment of service to others in need, no reasons were needed other than knowing that it was simply the right way.

Anyone reading this book expecting yet another scholarly work is looking in the wrong place, I am not a traditional scholar and this is not the kind of book one would expect to find in an academic setting. Nor am I a professional Christian, I have never worked for a Christian institution where one could automatically presume a level of shared understanding exists. I am a lifelong student and a "barefoot scholar", which is why this book may be totally discounted by many professional scholars, but I hope that is not the case. I make no apologies for any sins of omission, and readily admit to being selective as I pursued my personal quest for understanding. Jesus counseled us to be on guard against the scholars of the day, so I do not feel terribly guilty about being discriminatory about the scholarly sources I used.

Because this book is a personal quest for understanding it may be of some value to others who are embarking on their faith journey. It has taken me several decades to arrive at this point, having invested a huge amount of time trying to understand what it means to be a Christian in a challenging world, and why it matters at all.

Having embarked on my personal mission, my search for truth, I first approached the problem in the very traditional and conventional way that was provided by my church. I was astounded to find that there were no satisfactory answers to many of my questions, the veneer of faith was liberally applied over what seemed to me to be dubious concepts that I was supposed to accept. An explanation accompanied by a statement about having faith in what I was being told was not enough, I needed to know for myself and develop my own conclusions so I turned to books written by scholars. Often illuminating and always thought provoking, but too often accompanied by that same qualifier that you need to have faith to understand, which is tantamount to the author saying you have to trust me, have faith in me and believe what I am saying.

In conversation with an old friend mention was made of a minor Moslem sect that is being viciously persecuted as heretics. They follow the teachings of an Iman who advocated a return to the basic teachings of Mohammed, so that each worshiper could develop a personal relationship with Allah/God. This approach effectively invalidates much of the interpretive works that have been accumulated over the centuries, peeling back the Moslem faith to its very centre. Of course! What an obvious solution! Exactly the approach I needed to follow to understand what it means to be a Christian, go back to the words that Jesus spoke and study the essence of his teachings, blowing away the interpretive incrustations that has obscured the meaning for 20 centuries. Easier said than done.

As I kept peeling the onion that is called Christianity I discovered many blemishes that had been brushed over, issues that I thought too important to be ignored. Digging further, I found that the big questions that have haunted me for decades were also being asked by contemporary scholars, but for some reason these discussions were never communicated to the people in the congregations. For centuries the broader Christian community has, by and large, been served a heavily filtered, interpretive version that avoided the big questions and never acknowledged the impurities that I had found as I worked my way deeper into the Christian core. Sadly, this is still the case today across the Christian spectrum. I plodded on.

I am sure I am not alone in saying that several New Testament passages are often perplexing with respect to the words that are credited to Jesus. How often do you read a passage about compassion and then find something in the following verse that is a little brutal? Too often for me. It would be very easy to emulate Thomas Jefferson and simply cut and paste the passages to suit my purpose, but I am a student with a respect for empirical learning and know that such an approach would be self serving and dishonest.

The obvious place to find input from over 75 respected scholars from around the

Western world on this very issue is the Jesus Seminar, the 1985 study that went through all the words attributed to Jesus and attempted to identify those that represented his thoughts and ideas. The results of that almost five year study were reported in 'The Five Gospels', and that provided a starting point for my personal quest. The interpretive pieces and commentary contained in this illuminating work has been left behind, I simply overlaid the scriptural matrix on the Open Bible.

The theologians involved in the Jesus Seminar ranged from conservative to evangelical, covering the full spectrum of Christian perspectives. Unsurprisingly, this work was contentiously received when first published, and continues to be disputed by a large number of Christian believers and scholars. The primary criticism resulted because it attempted to separate and identify the words that were likely spoken by Jesus and his followers, thereby best representing the real teachings of Jesus.

They concluded that only a portion of the words attributed to Jesus in the Gospels met this criteria, suggesting that the others were written in by subsequent editors for a variety of reasons. In antiquity editors often embellished the work of prior writers in an attempt to bring clarity to a particular point, so we should not judge these editorial adjustments too harshly, as long as we remember that they exist.

Objections were raised with respect to the inclusion of the Gospel of Thomas because it is not included in the Bible, and therefore not valid, although scientific verification makes it very valid indeed. While the copy found with the Dead Sea Scrolls was written about the turn of the first century there is little doubt that it was a reproduction of a much earlier text.

Other complaints came from people who believe the Bible is the undisputed Word of God, and therefore is not open to question. This is not a view I share because my research has pointed too many times to human intervention in the development of the Bible, for distinctly human purposes. These sayings have been excluded as questionable because they appear to have a political basis that is very unlike the message Jesus was bringing, and these by and large are the parts of the Gospels that caused me so much anxiety in my youth.

In the second and third centuries the new church split into many factions, often accompanied by violent political upheaval. Textual edits were frequently made to push forward a particular agenda, they do not reflect the words or teachings of Jesus, nor do they have any basis in the mid first century Jesus Movement that propelled the spread of Christianity around the world.

This book looks at words that virtually everyone will agree were spoken by Jesus, and represent the position of the developing Jesus Movement in the four decades after Jesus died. I have gone to great lengths in my analysis to understand what kind of man Jesus was, what was his core message, and why his teachings had such a profound impact on the world. My observations and conclusions may offend some people, which I regret, my objective is not to offend, but to stimulate and encourage a re-examination of our faith in the millions of people who are funeral and wedding Christians.

Looking at Jesus' actions and the words that are universally agreed were spoken by Jesus, we can better understand the man and his message. When we look further into the teachings and beliefs of members of the

Jesus Movement in the first 40 years, the middle decades of the first century, our understanding improves. Presumably these early teachings would be based on a broader, more contemporary understanding of the words, actions and teachings of Jesus. Nevertheless, these have authenticity because they are thematically and philosophically tied to the undisputed words and actions of Jesus. This leads to the development of tentative conclusions and raises questions to challenge all of us in our personal quest. How is our Christian faith relevant in the 21st century?

I know I am not alone in my search, and hope that this work I have pulled together from many sources will be of help in your faith journey as you find your own way. If you disagree with my conclusions perhaps I have, at the very least, helped you reaffirm your own belief system.

Jerry Ford
Cobourg, Canada

The Really Big Questions

Each of us will have our own set of questions that matter most, but this is my list. If we tallied up all the questions that people could have the list would be pretty extensive, but that was not my objective; I wanted to know the answers to these three questions.

1. Jesus, his apostles and other followers were, through their faith, able to perform many miracles including healing the sick, casting out demons and bringing people back to life. This ability seems to have disappeared as that first generation died, not even Paul who was personally selected by Jesus to carry his message to the Gentiles had this power. What happened?

2. Who was this man Jesus and what was his real message, unembellished by the editors and revisionists of antiquity?

3. Why did this particular Jewish sect succeed in transforming the ancient world and survive through the ages to have a major formative influence on the development of Western civilization?

Timeline – The First Century

The universal dating system was calculated by the early church. They estimated the year of the birth of Jesus, which became year 0. We live in the Common Era, CE. BCE means Before Common Era.

4 BCE Birth of Jesus

26 John the Baptist begins his ministry

27 Jesus begins his ministry

30 Crucifixion of Jesus

33 Jewish persecution of the Jesus Movement begins

35 Conversion of Paul on the road to Damascus

39 Paul visits Peter in Jerusalem

44 Jewish persecution peaks

44 Martyrdom of James in Jerusalem

44 Peter imprisoned in Jerusalem and escaped

47 Paul's first missionary journey

50 Reconciliation of Peter and Paul

50 Council of Jerusalem allowing Gentiles to join the Jesus Movement and become followers of The Way

50 'The Two Ways' developed, later incorporated in the Didache

51 Paul's second missionary journey

53 Paul's third missionary journey

57 Letter to the Romans written

60 Paul in prison in Rome

64 Peter crucified in Rome

68 Martyrdom of Paul in Rome

70 Gospel of Mark written in Rome

70 Jewish revolt is put down and the Romans destroy the Temple in Jerusalem

70 Concept of the Holy Trinity theological discussion begins to gain momentum

80 Gospel of Matthew written for a Jewish audience

90 John exiled on the island of Patmos

90 Gospel of Luke and Acts of the Apostles written for Roman readers

95 Gospel of John written

Second century events of importance

120 The final version of the Didache

175 Irenaeus wrote 'Against Heresies"

1 – Setting the Scene

Judea – A Brief History

Jerusalem is only 300 miles from Alexandria, Egypt and just a long days' journey west of the overland trade route that formed the eastern border of Judea, connecting the road from Egypt with many of the land trade routes north and east of the Mediterranean. This had been a well traveled commercial pathway from before the beginning of recorded history. It was a magnet for brigands who could not resist the attraction of all this wealth passing through the hilly area, making travel in this section particularly dangerous for merchants and their caravans. Judea with its capital city of Jerusalem was no obscure backwater, it was right in the middle of a very important trade route and would definitely have enjoyed a steady stream of foreign visitors full of exotic stories, ideas and information.

In the middle of the sixth century BCE David was a benevolent monarch under which the Hebrew culture blossomed in every sense. His strong army and fortifications made the trade routes safer, and Jerusalem became a major trading centre. After his death, his son Solomon spent lavishly on Temples and residences, leaving the tiny kingdom without the resources to defend itself from its aggressive neighbours. Early in the fifth century BCE the country was subjugated by the Assyrians. This marked the end of political independence for the small Hebrew state and heralded the first of two major exiles that decimated the very well educated and cosmopolitan cultural elite of Jewish society. The Assyrians forcibly relocated prominent citizens and business people from Jerusalem to a number of centres in Assyria, where they eventually became absorbed by the local culture and lost their Hebrew identity and faith.

The structural legacy developed over the centuries, and fine tuned by David, consisted of two layers of government representing the secular and religious centres of power. The civil laws of the nation were the rules of the Hebrew faith as laid down in the Old Testament, and were enforced by the officers of the Temple, the group that evolved into the Pharisees of the early first century CE. Issues such as security and taxation were left to the secular government. This national structure was ahead of its time, providing a moral control over the population by the Temple officers as well as physical control through the secular army.

As conquerors, the Assyrians quickly realized the advantages of this dual control mechanism and established the secular government as a vassal of the Assyrian nation. Successive conquerors continued to follow this practice well into the fourth century CE, when the Roman Empire disintegrated.

Later in the fifth century BCE the Babylonians overthrew the Assyrians and initiated the second exile of Hebrew people into Babylon, but these unwilling migrants were able to retain their unique faith and culture. Many of their descendants eventually returned to Jerusalem after the Babylonian Empire was overthrown.

The Macedonian invasion led by Alexander the Great resulted in the development of a great commercial empire stretching from Alexandria in Egypt to the mountains of Greece. The legacy of this invasion lasted for hundreds of years, the adoption of Greek as the language of business had a major impact on the development of trade. For the first time in recorded history there was a common language that could be understood from one end of the Empire to the other. Greek remained the dominant, universal language from Egypt to Central Europe for seven centuries.

As the Macedonian Empire faded into oblivion after the death of Alexander the entire Middle East was enveloped in a century of conflict as various groups fought for control. The fleets of the Roman Empire quickly filled the void left by the Macedonians, and by 200 BCE they had total control of the Eastern Mediterranean Sea lanes. In 63 BCE Rome annexed the overland trade route and once again the Hebrew territory became a satellite state of a greater power. Herod the Great became the puppet leader accountable to Rome in 37 BCE.

When Herod died, about the same time Jesus was born, the state was divided among his sons, and the junior Herod was responsible for Judea and Jerusalem. After ten years of inept government the Romans established a system of prefects from Rome to be the final word in the three territories, the appointed prefect had absolute power. In 26 CE Pontius Pilate was installed as the prefect until he was recalled to Rome because his ferocity at subduing revolutionary activity was excessive even by Roman standards.

What was it really like for the people who lived in that place and time, Jerusalem circa 25 CE? Well, of course that would depend on your station in life, but we are not concerned with the social elite, we want to draw a picture of the lives of the common people who were first attracted to the message that Jesus had to deliver. The people who did not have enough to eat, the people who lived from pay to pay and for whom something like a broken bone could mean financial catastrophe.

Most families lived in a room or two that they rented, more if they could afford it. When they needed to relieve themselves they would empty the chamber pot in the streets or alternatively try and find somewhere private, perhaps a stable if they were lucky. The unpaved lanes between the buildings were narrow, always clogged with people, rotting refuse, animals and carts; the smells rising from the hardened earth only subsided in the rainy winter cold. The most pervasive thing no matter where you went was the smell, people and animals in close quarters, no sewers and no provision for people to wash themselves or their clothing.

All water came from centrally located wells and had to be carried home, reserved almost exclusively for drinking and food preparation, or ritual cleansing by the more devout Jews. The only redeeming feature was the weekly trash cart that passed at the end of the lane so householders could fill it with their garbage from the lane in front of their rooms. The refuse was then taken to the dump on the edge of town just outside the city walls. The garbage dump, Gehenna, was always burning because that was the only way to keep the overwhelming smell of decay under control.

A large part of the population were culturally Jewish, but did not practice their faith on a regular basis. To live as a devout Jew meant following the dietary laws, an expense that many of the people could not afford. For those who could afford it the Temple schools were very efficient at educating their sons, while the daughters remained at home learning how to be a dutiful wife and mother. From the day they are born the daughters were conditioned to defer to their brothers and commit to a life of servitude.

In some ways Jerusalem was unique as compared to other cities of antiquity, but in many respects it was much the same.

Because Jerusalem was the holy city and centre of the Jewish faith it was run in accordance with the Judaic laws. This religious infrastructure that had been in place for many centuries continued to be the dominant force for civil administration in the city and the surrounding countryside. For the Jewish population this control that emanated from the temple also dictated a strong moral code.

On the other hand, first century Jerusalem was a very cosmopolitan community simply because of its geographic placement between exotic Alexandria in Egypt and hedonistic, multicultural Antioch in the north. Like every community in the ancient and modern world the population was further subdivided into strata based on economics, their level of personal income and wealth. While the population was overwhelmingly Jewish there were also a number of pagan faith communities of which the two largest were the Greeks and Romans. Pagans were not restricted in practising their faith or maintaining their cultural identity.

The Temple tax collectors rarely bothered to approach the people in the poorer sections of the town because the pickings were so thin, but they did not hesitate to press the relatively more affluent members of the Jewish population. Of greater nuisance were the endless stream of beggars that greeted the passersby at every corner. The Roman Centurions who roamed the streets and squares at will were not much of a problem for the general population, but they were always a danger if they happened upon an unattended woman in an area where witnesses were easily intimidated into silence.

The Roman prefect had an agreement with the main synagogue, as long as the Temple police maintained order his soldiers would not engage in the pursuit of rape and pillage that were the normal spoils of war. The Roman soldiers were acting as an occupying army, a pretty quiet role for battle hardened veterans who would prefer to be getting more action and the opportunity to enjoy the fruits of their conquests, rather than sitting quietly as an occupying police force.

There are several other pertinent pieces of information that are important to understanding what life was like in Judea and the Hebrew culture in the early first century.

1. After centuries of oppression the Jewish people were looking for the

Messiah, the promised soldier who would destroy the oppressors and re-establish the grandeur of the time of David. They were not looking for a philosopher; the countryside was full of itinerant prophets who were generally left alone by the authorities unless they presented a military threat. Announcing that you were the Messiah was tantamount to a military call to arms, the messianic title was only conferred on Jesus by his followers after his death.

2. Archaeological evidence has shown that 40% of the population in the Roman Empire suffered from malnutrition, so slaves and landless peasants without a trade were undoubtedly always hungry. These are the people to whom Jesus first reached out to develop his following.

3. The average longevity for people living in the Roman Empire who survived childhood (five years) was about 40 years.

4. In Hebrew society men could marry after the age of 13 and were expected to be married by the time they were 18. Rabbis had to be married before they would be taken

seriously and an unmarried man would be considered an oddity with no credibility in the eyes of the people or Temple leaders. Jesus was over 30, considered to be a rabbi and had credibility, otherwise he would not have been allowed to read Scripture in the synagogue. He most certainly would have been married and may well have had children before he began his ministry.

5. The prefect, in this case Pontius Pilate, had absolute powers to control revolutionary activity and was accountable only to the Roman hierarchy for his actions. Leaders of the Temple and Herod were subordinates to his rule. Pilate was the opposite of a kindly ruler, he had a well earned reputation as a brutal man who eventually was recalled to Rome and held to account for his excessive brutality in putting down a Samaritan revolt.

6. Jesus was first and foremost a practising member of the Jewish faith. He knew the scriptures in detail, was deeply committed to upholding the Hebrew law in every

way, going to great lengths to satisfy the requirements of the sacred writings. He was determined to reform the Hebrew faith in terms that recognized the reality of the time in which he lived, he was not interested in creating a new religion. Until the destruction of the Temple in 70 CE, 40 years after the crucifixion of Jesus, the Jesus Movement was an offshoot sect of the Jewish faith.

7. In antiquity it was common practice for a scribe or acolyte to amend the work that had been written by a previous scholar, sometimes to correct errors but most frequently to edit or add content to the document. This was seen as an elaboration on the intent of the original writer, the editor would become nameless, and the work would go forward under the name of the original author. Isaiah is a perfect example of this, scholars have identified three distinct writers although the entire book is credited to Isaiah.

In this tradition the works of the original synoptic Gospel writers, Mark, Matthew and Luke, were amended in the second and third centuries to reflect values that were not present when the Gospels were written. This practice ended in the early fourth century when the Council of Nicaea codified the Bible and its contents.

Using the New Testament Sources

Of necessity we must rely on the synoptic Gospels of Matthew, Mark and Luke/Acts for the story of Jesus, simply because that is substantially all that is available to us. Other contemporary writing and historical records verify the bare facts but they do not provide us with any detailed information about the man, his teachings, or his devoted followers that carried his message across the known world within two centuries.

These Gospels were written after the fact, long after the fact if we apply our modern conceptual criteria about time, and they were often used for specific purposes that are more a reflection of the time they were written rather than the time Jesus lived. An additional problem exists because of the tendency to amend/correct what is written, a technique that was used to their advantage by the early church fathers as they molded the faith in the direction they thought it should be going.

Our objective is to capture the spirit of the time in which Jesus walked the earth and the four decades following his crucifixion. To do that we must try and eliminate the accumulated insights that have been added to the original story, these notes that follow are intended to help you understand and accept the rationale that has been applied. The Gospels are not being discounted in any way, we need look into their components in an effort to understand the time before the Gospels were written.

The Jesus Movement/The Way was growing rapidly at the expense of the Jewish faith and many of the pagan groups, but that was happening at some cost. The movement was being pulled in several directions fueled by differences of opinion on interpretation, however there were two distinct factions that prevailed. One was led by Peter the disciple and James the brother of Jesus, the conservative traditionalists based in Jerusalem. Peter and James began their work shortly after the crucifixion and believed that followers of Jesus must also conform to the Judaic laws, in effect they continued to view the movement as an extension of the Jewish faith. Paul appeared on the scene five or six years later and disagreed with this approach, he went to Jerusalem to meet with Peter and James to resolve the matter but they apparently quickly agreed to disagree.

Fourteen years after the crucifixion the on again, off again persecution by the Jewish establishment of the followers of The Way, encouraged and supported by the Romans, peaked. James was executed and Peter was imprisoned, but later escaped. Six years later Peter was back in Jerusalem where the Jesus Movement was once again being tolerated, and the divergent views between Peter and Paul were reconciled. Gentiles were now being welcomed into the emerging faith.

Paul, the fervent evangelist who had never met Jesus while he was living, experienced the risen Jesus on the road to Damascus and was converted to the new faith. While Peter and James centred the new movement around the Temple in Jerusalem Paul was actively promoting the faith in other communities, teaching that Jesus had liberated all people from the burdensome requirements of the Judaic laws in what we now know as the Old Testament. Paul established congregations of the faithful overseen by bishops and wrote a number of letters that eventually became an integral and very important part of the Bible. The first Christians would have known of Paul's teachings and opinions, although his letters were not copied and widely distributed until after his martyrdom in Rome in 68 CE, after the formative years that is the subject of our study.

At the time Matthew wrote his Gospel he would have had access to a large number of the Pauline letters, which is evident in his writing. His Gospel was directly addressed to his fellow Jews but it was obliquely targeted at the Gentiles as well, anyone reading his words would find them welcoming and uplifting. About a decade later the Gospel of Luke was intended for the Gentile audience so it accordingly reflected even more of Paul's philosophy. The perspective provided by Paul would not have had a significant impact in the formative first four decades of the Jesus Movement, and so it needs to be disregarded as we try and reconstruct the world of the first Christians.

The Gospel of Mark

Although Mark is included as the second Gospel in the Bible it was actually the first to be written, and there are some notable differences between Mark, Matthew and Luke. Mark was simply setting out the facts for clarity and probably best represents the known facts that were accepted by the first Christians. Mark contains no references to the life of Jesus before he appeared at the

Jordan River to meet John and be baptized. That entire section in Matthew (chapters 1 and 2) about Jesus' early life, and its subsequent embellishment by Luke, is a fabricated account designed to appeal to Matthew's intended audience, his fellow Jews.

Another very interesting thing about the Gospel of Mark, the original stopped at what we know as Chapter 16 verse 7 with no mention of the resurrection. The early church fathers excused this rather embarrassing situation by saying that the last pages of Mark's Gospel had been lost, and early in the second century set out to "correct" the text, adding what we now refer to as Mark 16, 8-20, a revision which over time became accepted as authentic. Given the manner in which documents were written in the first century it was almost impossible to cleanly lose the end of the document. Mark's Gospel was written in Rome and undoubtedly would have been very quickly copied many times for distribution to the faithful, it is obvious that the resurrection story was never part of Mark's Gospel. Does that mean that it should be ignored in terms of our analysis of first century Christian beliefs?

Absolutely not! Within a few days of the crucifixion a large number of people had experienced the resurrection firsthand, and that certainly would have fueled an incredible amount of gossip and speculation in the streets of Jerusalem. One can be sure that the Romans and the leaders of the Temple would have done everything in their power to discredit the resurrection story, and they did not succeed. We can very safely presume that the resurrection story was well entrenched as a fundamental truth in the minds of the members of the Jesus Movement within a year of the crucifixion, to the point where it was a certainty. No discussion required, it happened and it is up to each of us to accept that truth if we are to understand the mindset of the first believers, those who were truly the living, early roots of Christianity.

We must remember that Mark was writing simply to record the facts as he knew them. His target audience was the followers of The Way, and other Jews and the Roman population were understandably skeptical about the resurrection claims. Mark must have been sensitive to the possibility that his writing might be used against his fellow believers if he pushed the story too far, choosing instead to stick to the well documented facts. This position is supported by Mark's failure to ascribe responsibility for the death of Jesus to anyone other than Pontius Pilate, a man who was discredited many years before Mark wrote.

The most complete summary we have of the resurrection can be found in Luke, where he built his narrative around the oral tradition that would have been preserving the resurrection stories from the time of their occurrence until Luke put quill to parchment. The oral tradition was still very alive and reliable when Luke wrote his Gospel, and any deficiencies or stretching of the truth would have attracted attention immediately. Several independent, contemporary manuscripts support the authenticity of Luke's rendering, so the omission of the resurrection story by Mark supports this postulation.

The Gospel of Mark is the earliest surviving written record of the teachings of Jesus and it became one of the foundational pieces for the other Gospels that were written. It is the best example we have of the basic beliefs of the first members of the Jewish sect that were later labeled Christians.

The Gospel of Matthew

The Gospel of Matthew was written about the year 80 CE, which is some 50 years after the crucifixion. It is highly unlikely that this is the same tax collector Matthew who was the disciple, but it was certainly written by a first or second generation member of the Jesus Movement. This Gospel was specifically targeted at the Judaic community, designed to convince the Jewish people that Jesus was in fact the Messiah. We must remember that Matthew was a committed believer who was determined to provide a palatable path that other Jews could follow to accept the teachings of Jesus, we need to admire his zealous approach because he did a wonderful job of accomplishing his goal. In reading his words, however, we need to seriously consider the spiritual message he is delivering and not pay too much attention to the literal interpretation.

Toward that end Matthew went to great length to create a back story for Jesus that was consistent with the prophecies in the sacred writings that we now refer to as the Old Testament. His purpose was to legitimize Jesus to his fellow Jews, and the first two chapters of his Gospel do a fine job of creating authenticity in a manner that would be entirely credible to the Jewish population in the first century. There are two prophecies that were indisputably fulfilled by Jesus and were not inventions, he was from Nazareth and was of the house of David. The other prophecies Matthew has managed to creatively incorporate into Jesus's history include:

- The virgin birth
- Born in Bethlehem
- Great people would herald his birth
- Called Emmanuel – God with us
- He was called out of Egypt

Matthew was a Jewish scholar, a follower of The Way, who wanted to share the good news with his community and thereby legitimize his beliefs in the minds of the Hebrew people. The movement was still in its gestation phase, newly evolved from just being a sect of the Jewish religion, a faith that was under considerable pressure since the Jerusalem Temple had been destroyed by the Romans a decade earlier. This disruption created an unprecedented opportunity for recruitment among the Jewish population to join the new movement, and that was Matthew's goal.

The Gospel of Luke

A few years later when Luke sat down to write his very well crafted Gospel, which was addressed to the Roman Gentile community, he had several documents that he could draw on. The lost writings that recorded the savings of Jesus referred to as 'Q' by modern scholars, the very reliable oral tradition that had its origins in the Hebrew faith, the historical account provided by Mark and the much glossier production that Matthew had developed for a predominantly Jewish audience. The existence and content of all these documents were well known to contemporary scholars, Luke would have been hard pressed to develop a Gospel that differed substantially from the previous writings, in particular those of Matthew, who exercised considerable license in setting the scene for Jesus to be the one spoken of in so many ancient Hebrew prophecies.

As a result, Luke had to pick up many of the fabrications made by Matthew so that the story continued in a way that would resonate with the followers. That does not mean that Luke agreed with these conjectures but, unless they seriously offended his sensitivities and were simply omitted from his narrative, he slavishly repeated them.

We are concerned here with the understanding that the first and second generation members of the expanding Christian sect within the Jewish faith would have, and these sections of Matthew and Luke postdate our period of study. That does not in any way imply that they are invalidated in the larger picture, but they simply do not relate to the objectives of this work, consequently they have been ignored so that we can have a better understanding of what the first and second generation Christian community believed.

The Gospel of John

The Gospel of John is a retelling of the stories contained in Matthew, Mark and Luke in a mystical, spiritual way that is more representative of the Jewish mystical tradition that was common among the Jewish sect known as the Essenes. It is full of imagery and poetic beauty, an expression of spirituality at its finest, but it is not a source for factual information.

Acts of the Apostles

Acts was the second book written by Luke and really should be read immediately after the Gospel of Luke. It fits very nicely as a continuation of the history and faith story that is so well told in the closing chapters of Luke's Gospel. Our study of the first two generations of the Jesus Movement would not be complete without inclusion of the material covered in the early chapters of the book of Acts. This book contains a large amount of factual historical material that directly impacts our field of interest, an invaluable source for our purposes.

The Nazarene

No records exist of the first 30 years of Jesus' life, but that is no surprise because he was just another Jewish child being raised in an intensely Jewish society. Growing up in the small town of Nazareth was not the same as growing up in the more cosmopolitan Jerusalem that had so many worldly distractions, so we can be sure that Jesus had a very conventional Jewish upbringing.

His father was a carpenter and it appears that Jesus was the first child of many, which means that he would have been working with his father from a very early age to learn his trade. Having a skilled trade meant that Jesus and his family, although landless peasants, were not at the bottom rung of the social ladder. They could afford a decent education for their sons at the local synagogue and would participate in regular pilgrimages to the synagogue in Jerusalem, the spiritual centre of the Hebrew faith.

Jesus was undoubtedly a prodigy which would have made him a favoured student in the synagogue. In his ministry he demonstrated a level of knowledge and understanding that suggests very strongly that he had an excellent mentor within the synagogue to help him develop his prescription for revolutionizing the Judaic faith. Was that mentor a man or men of God, or God? We will never know for sure, and this becomes a point of faith for followers of The Way in the first century and the 21st century.

Jesus was a devout Jew and lived a life in accordance with the Scriptures and social norms of the times in his Judaic community. He would likely have been married at a relatively early age, and in the normal course of events would have had a family that he would have supported through his trade. Jesus apparently did not have any adult children, if he did they would have been at his side during the crucifixion. There is strong, albeit circumstantial, evidence that Mary Magdalene might have been his wife.

Jesus may have begun to identify with his messianic role very early in his life, but that does not appear to be the case. When Jesus had begun his ministry he returned to Nazareth with his message and was badly received, his behaviour as a teacher and prophet was not consistent with the nature of the man who had grown up with them, lived in their community and they knew well. Something happened to Jesus between the time he left his family in Nazareth and was baptized by John, something that galvanized him and set him on his mission. Did he spend some time among the Essenes, the mystical Judaic sect? Numerous scholars have pointed out that the philosophy expressed by Jesus in his ministry suggests that he may have been influenced by their teachings, and that is certainly supported by the emphasis on communal property that was at its earliest stages a fundamental part of life for followers of The Way.

Did Jesus set out to satisfy the scriptural prophecies because he was driven as a man to do so, or was he following the instructions that he had received from God? Another question for which we will never know the answer but which will be integral to the faith experience for many followers. This is where many modern day critics relying on our still imperfect understanding of how our minds work will have a field day. My personal view is that it does not matter, at this stage in Jesus' life we have so many other larger issues to consider as we look at his actions as the Son of Man, and later as he assumed his role as the Son of God. Simply put, it is a matter of faith.

The man who left Nazareth underwent a life changing experience as he wandered the countryside before he appeared at the Jordan River to be baptized by John. The man from Nazareth who was a descendent of David had an encounter with God that convinced him that he was the chosen one. A Messiah not of the sword but of the heart, whose role was to minister to the Jewish people and get them back on the path that God intended for his chosen people.

2 - The Spoken Words

Linguistic scholars have determined that a single original source document was used for the words spoken by Jesus in the Gospels of Matthew, Mark and Luke. This document, conveniently referred to as 'Q', unfortunately has never been located but its existence is unquestioned because of the patterns of speech and thematic consistency. With the 1956 discovery of the Nag Hammabi scrolls in a cave in the hills of Judea the 'Q' theory was further substantiated by the collaborating evidence found. The Gospel of Thomas, a document that had been lost to the world for 1900 years, was written in the ancient format containing quotations without narrative, and many of them were the same as those found in the Gospels of Matthew, Mark and Luke.

Since this master document 'Q' is not available scholars needed to use a number of analytical tools to try to determine what was actually said by Jesus and what was later attributed to Jesus by another author for any one of several reasons. In 1985 a project was begun with the involvement of 76 noted biblical scholars from around the western world in what became a five year in depth analysis of every spoken word that was attributed to Jesus in the Bible and the Gospel of Thomas. Upon completion the Jesus Seminar members published a number of books about their findings which created huge controversy, particularly among those who view the Bible as exclusively God's word. The study premise was empirically sound and is functionally the best analysis of its kind that has ever been done, attempting to separate the original material from the interpretive works of man.

The Gospels contain many more sayings that have been attributed to Jesus than are included in this listing. The sayings that are listed here are only those that the Jesus Seminar Scholars determined were spoken by Jesus, or could have been spoken by Jesus, based on their context and theme. Although there will be objections raised because of the omission of those sayings and teachings in the Gospels that have been attributed to Jesus but did not make the cut, no one will argue that anything included in this listing does not belong here. Our objective is to learn more about the kind of person Jesus was and why his teachings were so quickly accepted and carried around the world by his disciples and followers, therefore in this chapter we must concentrate on only those words that had been indisputably or likely have been spoken by Jesus himself.

Throughout the Gospels the words of Jesus are repeated many times and, to permit us to undertake an analytical review, these sayings of Jesus have been organized by topics. There are no verse references in the text although chapter and verse references have been provided at the beginning of the quoted passage to facilitate your review. The original Gospels were not written with chapter and verse references, that was a 15th century innovation after the development of the printing press, which enabled the increasingly literate population to read the Scriptures themselves. Quoting a specific verse out of context will often lead to confusion and misunderstanding, so sayings are presented in the Gospel context where possible. The text used is from the Open Bible that is readily available on the Internet, the reader is encouraged to use any translation you prefer so you can interpret the subject matter in a manner that you find most comfortable.

The nitty gritty detail of what each of us believe as people of faith is of secondary importance in the grand scheme of things, what matters most is that we each understand and take ownership of our personal value system in a manner that is consistent with our faith. Western society has been developed around Christian ideals and structures, perhaps to an extent that is excessive and in need of change as our culture becomes more cosmopolitan, but that is the reality today. There are many people who choose to live without religious convictions, tailoring their lives around moral precepts that are the underpinnings of our society. They choose to live by default and, because the morality that they accept is rooted in Christian teachings, they are defaulting into a Christian lifestyle without ever having thought about it.

If we live deliberately our lives are much more satisfying. To live deliberately we need to have a game plan and the starting place for that game plan is a firm understanding about our personal values. Can you truthfully answer these questions?

- What do you believe?
- What do you hold sacred?
- How far can you be pushed to compromise your values before you say *enough!*?
- What is your role in this life that you have been given?
- Are you the person you appear to be?

Jesus lived a very deliberate life, he knew exactly where he was going and how he was going to get there. This analysis is part of my journey as I try and follow the same path. Long ago I accepted the basic framework of the Christian faith as exemplified in our society, but I needed to go deeper and better understand my faith as I attempted to better understand myself. This analysis is certainly not definitive but it is my analysis, offered to you to encourage you to undertake your own faith journey and determine what it is that you believe, and why.

Beatitudes

On the first reading these passages seem to be fairly straightforward, words of comfort to the many who are hurting in this world. Closer comparison with other words that Jesus spoke brings up a number of questions however, and suggests that these sayings were addressed separately to a specific audience and, because of the common element of compassion they demonstrate, have been compiled as a unit by Matthew and Luke in what may well be a contrived setting.

Jesus said a great deal about what the Kingdom of God/Heaven was like, and the overwhelming tone of his message was that heaven is here on earth and within each of us, he never described it as some ethereal place where souls will rest in blissful perpetuity. For that matter, he never mentioned hell in the catastrophic way that purposely was extrapolated by the early church fathers to intimidate an impoverished, unhappy population with false promises/threats of being rewarded in heaven or punished forever. Were these passages we refer to as the Beatitudes largely the result of appealing to the masses so that Jesus could build the critical mass he needed to carry out his mission?

Matthew created an environment where these were pulled together as part of a single speaking event, although they are more likely to have been a number of separate statements made by Jesus through the three years of his ministry. We were only able to identify words of Jesus that represent the sayings in Matthew 3-6, but the other sayings to verse 11 do fit well thematically, and we can be quite certain that they do represent the beliefs of the early Christians.

When compared to the scriptural accounts you will find that the Gospels contain far more dialogue for Jesus than has been used in this study. It appears that there were a number of editorial additions and changes by later New Testament revisionists for several different reasons. In many cases they were well intended elaborations on the Christian principles as interpreted by the early theologians. In some cases, these revisions appear to have a much less enlightening purpose, were they designed to keep the common people content with their lot in life by promising a heavenly reward? Did they purposely emphasize the existence of hell as a place of punishment to emphasize the cost of nonadherence? Whatever the reason for their creation, these mechanisms that served to influence and control the Christian community were enshrined in the Gospels before the Bible as we know was concretized by the Council of Nicaea in 325 CE.

Matthew 5, 3-4
Blessed are the poor in spirit, for theirs is the kingdom of heaven. Blessed are the mourners, for they will be comforted.

Matthew 5, 6

Blessed are those who hunger and thirst for righteousness, for they will be satisfied.

Luke 6, 20
Blessed are you who are poor, for yours is the kingdom of God.

Luke 6, 21
Blessed are you who hunger now, for you will be satisfied.
Blessed are you who weep now, for you will laugh.

Thomas 54
Blessed are the poor, for yours is the kingdom of heaven.

Thomas 69, 2
Blessed are the hungry, for the belly of him who desires will be filled

.

Jesus clearly understood the concerns of the common people, he had spent the first 30 years of his life in that environment and pragmatically endeavoured to fill that void as he expanded his base of followers. This suggests that these sayings arose early in his ministry and were later expanded upon in other sayings that are credited to Jesus. They are often repeated in a somewhat different form, but that only makes sense.

Anyone delivering the same message several times as Jesus did will use different phraseology, but essentially say the same thing.

Beware the Scholars

In the early first century the Temple priests were the experts at interpreting the scripture and scriptural interpretation was the law, the Temple law that effectively governed the social and cultural aspects of the Jewish world. The priestly class called the Pharisees were keepers of the law and to challenge their interpretation and decisions was almost heresy. The Pharisees were based in and controlled the Jerusalem synagogue which was the spiritual center of the Jewish faith, which gave them de facto control over the hearts and minds of all devout Judaic people. They also enjoyed a privileged and powerful position in the court of the Roman puppet Herod Antipas, where they exerted considerable influence. The Temple tax that was levied against everyone went to the synagogue and the Pharisees were able to live in comfortable luxury by comparison to the average Judean.

Jesus was critical of the Pharisees for several reasons, the fact that they lived well on the backs of the common people with whom Jesus could identify so closely was certainly adequate justification, but he also found their positions hypocritical and had no compulsion against saying so. The Hebrew faith has a tradition of being charitable to the less fortunate and yet it appears the Pharisees reveled in making judgments on others behaviour while being self serving in their devotion to duty. They were the elite, more comfortable in the courts of Herod than the streets of the city that were crowded with the disenfranchised and ill. The distain that Jesus felt is plainly apparent in his words.

Matthew 23, 5-7
All their actions are done to attract attention. They widen their phylacteries, and increase the size of their tassels, and like to have the place of honour at dinner, and the best seats in the Synagogues, and to be greeted in the markets with respect, and to be called 'Rabbi' for everybody.

Mark 12, 38-39
See that you are on your guard against the teachers of the law, who delight to walk about in long robes, and to be greeted in

the streets with respect, and to have the best seats in the Synagogues, and places of honour at dinner.

Luke 11, 43
Alas for you Pharisees! You delight to have the front seat in the Synagogues, and to be greeted in the markets with respect.

Luke 20, 46
Be on your guard against the teachers of the law, who delight to walk about in long robes, and like to be greeted in the streets with respect, and to have the best seats in the Synagogues, and places of honour at dinner.

These passages are very clear indications that the man Jesus of Nazareth had a temper, and was very capable of becoming angry about those things that offended him. He had no patience for hypocrisy, and took great exception to seeing privileged people take advantage of others because of their social standing. His disdain for fine garments while the general population dressed in coarse, drab materials is evident in his remarks. He was a man who valued intangibles over the material aspects of life.

Charity

Charity is a concept that is endemic to the Judaic faith. Since the earliest Christians were all Jewish they had no difficulty understanding what Jesus was referring to, there was no need to state the obvious, particularly when he so clearly demonstrated it by living charitably in his own life. It is therefore understandable that Jesus said very little directly about charity, the Jewish principal of being charitable was automatically extended to the emerging Christian sect. Unsurprisingly, Christian organizations have had a huge impact on the development of charities and the completion of charitable works from the first century until today. The words and actions of Jesus were primary drivers for the first generation of Christians, who were simply building on their Judaic tradition.

This is one of those situations that demonstrates very clearly the value of the oral tradition and reliance on established social and religious customs. Our modern approach demands that we see proof, something in writing, whereas in antiquity customs and traditions that defined a society were simply accepted. Relying on the evidence we have available helps us greatly, but undoubtedly there are many lost words and teachings of Jesus and his disciples, as well as established but unwritten mores, that were available to the early Christian community. At the very least, we can safely presume that the oral tradition passed down by the people of The Way reliably reflects the values that Jesus demonstrated in his own life.

There is a close and very strange relationship between Jesus' approach to charity and persons with wealth. Time and again he stresses the inability of the rich to enter the kingdom of heaven, and exhorts them to sell all they have and give it to the poor as you see in this quotation from Mark. *There is still one thing wanting in you; go and sell all that you have, and give to the poor, and you will have wealth in heaven; then come and follow me.*

On the other hand, Jesus was often the beneficiary of those with riches even to the point where his tomb was provided by a rich supporter, Joseph of Arimathea. It seems that Jesus was troubled by the very human conflict that we all have encountered, where do you draw the line between charity and protecting your own self interest to ensure your survival?

Matthew 6, 3
But, when you do acts of charity, do not let your left hand know what your right hand is doing,

Mark 10, 20
There is still one thing wanting in you; go and sell all that you have, and give to the poor, and you will have wealth in heaven; then come and follow me.

Luke 6, 30
Give to everyone who asks of you;

In this famous parable of the Good Samaritan Jesus crosses the sectarian border of the time and introduces the concept that compassion for people is an integral component of acts of charity, and that compassion goes beyond the boundaries of race and creed.

Luke 10, 30-35
A man was once going down from Jerusalem to Jericho when he fell into the hands of robbers, who stripped him of everything, and beat him, and went away leaving him half dead. As it chanced, a

priest was going down by that road. He saw the man, but passed by on the opposite side. A Levite, too, did the same; he came up to the spot, but, when he saw the man, passed by on the opposite side. But a Samaritan, traveling that way, came upon the man, and, when he saw him, he was moved with compassion. He went to him and bound up his wounds, dressing them with oil and wine, and then put him on his own mule, and brought him to an inn, and took care of him. The next day he took out two silver coins and gave them to the innkeeper. 'Take care of him,' he said, 'and whatever more you may spend I will myself repay you on my way back.'

Thomas 62, 2
Do not let your left hand know what your right hand is doing.

Conflict

We will see many accounts in the Gospels about Jesus actively courting confrontation, but they were in specific situations where he perceived an injustice existed and set out to remedy it. He always chose his time and place very well, following his own advice to the disciples to act wisely.

In the following passages it is interesting to note that Jesus was not presuming that the recipient of his advice might win the case. To properly understand this position, we must consider the environment in the Judea in which Jesus grew up and lived his life. He, like so many others in the lower social classes, was landless, one of many skilled labourers that worked for hire. In the social hierarchy of the day these workers were not far from the bottom and the likelihood that they would prevail over the claims of a higher status merchant or landowner were undoubtedly slim, so his advice to be conciliatory was simply a tool for survival.

Matthew 5, 25-26
Be ready to make friends with your opponent, even when you meet them on your way to the court; otherwise they might hand you over to the judge, and the judge to the judicial officer, and you will be thrown into prison. I tell you, you will not come out until you have paid the last cent.

Luke 12, 58-59
When, for instance, you are going with your opponent before a magistrate, on your way to the court do your best to be quit of him; otherwise he might drag you before the judge, then the judge will hand you over to

the bailiff of the court, and the bailiff throw you into prison. You will not, I tell you, come out until you have paid the very last cent.

Matthew 5, 39-42
But I say to you that you must not resist those who wrong you; but, if anyone strikes you on the right cheek, turn the other to them also. If someone sues you for your shirt, let them have your cloak as well. If you are forced to carry a soldier's pack for one mile, carry it two. Give to anyone who asks and, if someone wants to borrow from you, do not turn them away.

Luke 6, 29
When someone gives one of you a blow on the cheek, offer the other cheek as well; when anyone takes away your cloak, do not keep back your coat either.

Jesus' intelligent assessment of the reality of life is obvious as it is everywhere in the Gospels, he was a very smart man. It is clear that he was not the revolutionary Messiah that so many of his countrymen were praying for, recognizing that calling the common people to rebel against the Roman legionnaires would be a formula for a bloody disaster. He developed a strategy to survive in a hostile environment, something that is reflected in other places such as his comments about rendering to Caesar that which is Caesar's and to God that which is God's.

Criticizing Others

Jesus is admonishing us to concentrate on looking within ourselves so that we can purge our own impurities, rather than concentrating on the imperfections of others.

Matthew 7, 3-5
Why do you look at the speck of sawdust in your friend's eye, while you pay no attention at all to the plank of wood in yours? How will you say to your friend 'Let me take out the speck from your eye,' when all the time there is a plank in your own? Hypocrite! Take out the plank from your own eye first, and then you will see clearly how to take out the speck from your friend's.

Luke 6, 37
Do not judge, and you will not be judged; do not condemn, and you will not be condemned. Forgive, and you will be forgiven.

Thomas 26, 1-2

You see the mote in your brother's eye, but you do not see the beam in your own eye. When you cast the beam out of your own eye, then you will see clearly to cast the mote from your brother's eye.

Once again Jesus is telling us to point our finger towards our own chest and focus on what we find therein. Jesus clearly had a great deal of personal experience with reflective introspection, and recommends that we all concentrate on searching our souls so we can find ourselves, as a prerequisite to finding God.

Dealing with Authorities

As a vassal state of the Roman Empire Judea and its citizens had very little freedom of speech or assembly, and any activities that seemed remotely political would be subjected to harsh and immediate action. The Romans had a very effective remedy for crowd control called massacre, and they were not hesitant to use it.

Judea was unique in the Roman Empire of the time because it was ostensibly self ruling under Herod and his successive dynasties, but they were a puppet government who owed their allegiance to Rome. Why was Judea treated as a special case? There are two fundamental reasons, unlike most of the territories captured by the Romans Judea had an established, structured community that contained its own checks and balances so it was economically prudent for the Roman conquerors to leave that in place. Secondly, Rome had a pattern of letting conquered people retain their religion as long as it did not interfere with Rome's political ambitions. In Judea the established religious order was an integral part of community structure and leaving it intact provided an added measure of control over dissent.

From the Roman perspective everything was perfectly structured in Judea, the people were accustomed to being controlled by two levels of quasi-government (synagogue and the state), so the cost of policing their new territory would be very low for the Romans. Just as important was the existence of an established tax collection infrastructure, which meant that the Romans could exact tribute without having to do the collecting. While the citizens of Judea undoubtedly opposed this Roman occupation they fared substantially better than those areas that were subjugated by the swords of the Legionnaires.

Into this cauldron of grumbling dissent came Jesus, just one of the many itinerant preachers/prophets that had been prowling in the wilds of the Judean Hills for centuries. The Old Testament is full of the stories and teachings of the more prominent of these prophets like Ezra, Elijah, Ezekiel and Isaiah, often fueled by promises of a new order for God's chosen people.

Rome was content to let the Judeans dream all they liked about a coming Messiah as long as it did not interfere with business, prophets who crossed the line were martyred. Jesus clearly understood the rules of the game and adroitly stickhandled around the obstacles until he chose his day of reckoning. He counseled his followers to do the same, be as wise as a snake but innocent as a dove while paying Caesar what he is due as a conqueror. Solid common sense advice for surviving in a hostile environment.

Matthew 10, 16

So be as wise as snakes, and as blameless as doves.

Matthew 22, 21
Then pay to the Emperor what belongs to the Emperor, and to God what belongs to God.

Mark 12, 17
Pay to the Emperor what belongs to the Emperor, and to God what belongs to God.

Luke 20, 25
Well then, pay to the Emperor what belongs to the Emperor, and to God what belongs to God.

Thomas 39, 3
You, however, be as wise as serpents and as innocent as doves.

Thomas 100, 2
Give Caesar what belongs to Caesar, give God what belongs to God

Families

These passages are ones that I find uncomfortable, but they are understandable when viewed in the context that Jesus was living. He is saying what so many people down the ages have always found, kinship with your birth family generally is eclipsed as you mature. We develop our own family of like minded friends who share our values and better understand who we are in our heart. Jesus is pushing this to the full extent of that second tier family, he is on a quest that goes beyond our worldly concerns and anyone who shares that journey with him must be prepared to make the break with his past.

Matthew 12, 48-50
Who is my mother? And who are my brothers? Here are my mother and my brothers! For anyone who does the will of my Father who is in heaven is my brother and sister and mother.

Thomas 99, 2
Those here who do the will of my father are my brothers and my mother. It is they who will enter the kingdom of my father.

This next saying leaves me very cold for two reasons. I have a very loving and supportive family that encourages each of us to find our own way, and offers a refuge in times of trouble, to actively disown them is offensive. My second concern is the word 'hate'. I can understand being encouraged to hate evil but why should I be required to take such extreme action against those I love, people who, coincidentally, are also fellow travelers on the Christian path?

I wonder if these sayings were made in a particular situation where the context might mitigate the severity of the statement, and that contextual explanation has been lost so we are left with only the brutal end of the conversation? Or are we seeing the brittle edge of the conflict that Jesus had within himself as he progressed on his chosen journey to certain death?

Luke 14, 26
If any one comes to me and does not hate their father, and mother, and wife, and children, and brothers, and sisters, yes and even their life, he can be no disciple of mine.

Luke 17, 33
Whoever is eager to get the most out of their life will lose it; but whoever will lose it will preserve it.

Jesus was fully committed to his chosen path from the very beginning and was prepared to be very hard nosed in demanding that his followers make the same level of commitment. His tenacity and determination are without question, but why does he expect us all to make that level of commitment? Why should we throw our lives away and be prepared to die horribly for a cause, no matter how strong our faith? Most of us prefer to live a life of humility and service to what has evolved over the centuries as the Christian doctrine we have today. Jesus demanded total, unwavering commitment from his first century followers no matter what the cost. While many of these first Christians were prepared to make that commitment to the point of being martyred, I wonder how relevant this is for Christians in the 21st century?

Have and Have Not

From our 21st century vantage point where everything is about power and money, greed is the primary motivator around the globe. History shows that this is not simply a current trend, it is the way the world has always been and probably will continue to be. It is very difficult to make any sense of these sayings unless we consider that they are simply statements of fact. Was that what Jesus meant or was he delivering these lines the same way he gave us his parables?

Perhaps we should not be looking at these sayings in relevance to the material things in life, could it be that Jesus was speaking only about the spiritual aspect of our existence? Once we move away from our not so very modern automatic default, where value refers to an asset with a price, and substitute the concept of spiritual health and well being, these sayings take on a whole different meaning.

Mark 4, 25
For, to those who have, more will be given; while, from those who have nothing, even what they have will be taken away.

Luke 8, 18
Take care, then, how you listen. For, to all those who have, more will be given; while, from all those who have nothing, even what they seem to have will be taken away.

Luke 17, 33
Whoever is eager to get the most out of their life will lose it; but whoever will lose it will preserve it.

Thomas 41, 1-2
Whoever has something in his hand will receive more, and whoever has nothing will be deprived of even the little he has.

Instructions for Followers

The Gospel writers often put the instructive teachings of Jesus in a narrative that addresses the disciples, but it is very clear that they, in many respects, relate to the throng of followers as well as the chosen disciples. As an example, it is not what you eat that matters, it is what comes out of your mouth that is important. This message was clearly directed at the general population who were required by the synagogue hierarchy to follow the centuries old dietary laws. In a few words Jesus invalidates the position of the Pharisees, and then goes on to give them a veiled insult about the words they mouth, both of which resonate very well with his followers.

Following the dietary laws was very expensive, as it is today if you go to a kosher supermarket. Many of the poor could not afford to follow the dietary laws or make the sacrifices called for by the Temple, rendering them second class citizens. These words of Jesus validated their worth by discounting the dietary requirements of their faith, while at the same time mocking the self indulgent

Pharisees who lived in wealth at the expense of the poor.

This was very liberating news for the devout but poor members of the Jewish population who lived beyond the pale, not because they choose to but because there was no alternative for them. It is really no different than it has been in every society and culture in the past, present and undoubtedly will be in the future. People are summarily disenfranchised because they are in the wrong economic strata or social set, but are still intent on living a life of decency and respect. Is it any surprise that these people formed the voluminous core of the Jesus Movement?

Matthew 15, 10-11
Listen, and mark my words. It is not what enters a person's mouth that 'defiles' them, but what comes out from their mouth — that does defile them!

Mark 7, 14-15
Listen to me, all of you, and mark my words. There is nothing external to a person, which by going into them can 'defile' them; but the things that come out of a person are the things that defile them.

Thomas 14, 5

For what goes into your mouth will not defile you, but that which issues from your mouth - it is that which will defile you.

Matthew 8, 22

Follow me, and leave the spiritually dead to bury their dead.

Luke 9, 59-60

Follow me. Leave the spiritually dead to bury their dead; but go yourself and carry far and wide the news of the kingdom of God.

In the second half of the foregoing passage Jesus exhorts us to *'go yourself and carry far and wide the news of the kingdom of God,'* and the following sayings appear to be rules for being a good guest on the road.

Luke 10, 7

Remain at that same house, and eat and drink whatever they offer you;

That Luke 10, 8

Whatever town you visit, if the people welcome you, eat what is set before you;

Thomas 6, 5

Do not tell lies, and do not do what you hate, for all things are plain in the sight of heaven.

John the Baptist

One of the Old Testament prophecies concerning the coming Messiah was that he would be preceded by one who would herald his arrival. John the Baptist fulfilled this prophetic role for Jesus, paving the way for Jesus to be accepted by the common people as someone special, so much more than just another prophet. In the passages that follow Jesus makes fun of the Pharisees who have come to investigate the work and words of John the Baptist, something that would have been very well received by the common people in attendance and certainly would have been the subject of discussion wherever people congregated. Jesus was quick to capitalize on any opportunity to establish his position as he began his ministry, very pragmatic!

Matthew 11, 8
What did you go out into the wilderness to look at? A reed waving in the wind? If not, what did you go out to see? A man richly dressed? Why, those who wear rich things are to be found in the courts of kings!

Luke 7, 25

What did you go out into the wilderness to look at? A reed waving in the wind? If not, what did you go out to see? A man dressed in rich clothing? Why, those who are accustomed to fine clothes and luxury live in royal palaces.

Thomas 78, 1-2

Why have you come out into the desert? To see a reed shaken by the wind?

Kingdom of God/Heaven

There are more than 1800 words on this single topic in the Gospels that are indisputably directly attributable to Jesus, words he did say that are consistent with the message he delivered, and therefore have been identified as solid renditions of his teachings by biblical scholars. In 17 entries in the Gospels the subject is addressed in short statements and parables, sometimes they are repeated but that is not always the case. The most common repetitive saying concerns the mustard seed, something to which the followers could easily relate whereas something more obtuse (as we will see

74

later) lacked the simplicity of understanding provided by the mustard seed story.

When one reads through the text about what Jesus had to say about the Kingdom of God it is important to note that he never refers to palaces in the sky, all his illustrative stories paint the picture of a benign and patient patriarchal figure that are generally cast in terms that were relevant to the common people and their life experience. Jesus quite clearly points out that heaven is here on earth and within each of us, Luke 17, 20 – 21. This is carried a little further in the saying recorded by Thomas 113, 2 – 4, where Jesus says that heaven is scattered all over the earth and people do not see it.

Matthew 13, 31-33
The kingdom of heaven is like a mustard seed, which a person took and sowed in his field. This seed is smaller than all other seeds, but, when it has grown up, it is larger than the herbs and becomes a tree, so that the wild birds come and roost in its branches. The kingdom of heaven is like some yeast which a woman took and covered up in three pecks of flour, until the whole had risen.

Matthew 13, 44-46

The kingdom of heaven is like a treasure hidden in a field, which a person found and hid again, and then, in their delight, went and sold everything that they had, and bought that field.

Again, the kingdom of heaven is like a merchant in search of choice pearls. Finding one of great value, they went and sold everything that they had, and bought it.

Matthew 18, 23-34

Therefore, the kingdom of heaven may be compared to a king who wished to settle accounts with his servants. When he had begun to do so, one of them was brought to him who owed him ten thousand bags of gold; and, as he could not pay, his master ordered him to be sold towards the payment of the debt, together with his wife, and his children, and everything that he had. The servant threw himself down on the ground before him and said 'Have patience with me, and I will pay you all.' The master was moved with compassion; and he let him go, and forgave him the debt. But, on going out, that same servant came upon one of his fellow servants who owed him a hundred silver coins. Seizing him by the throat, he said 'Pay what you owe me.' His fellow servant threw himself on the ground and begged for mercy. 'Have patience with me,' he said, 'and I will pay you.' But the other would not, but went and put him in prison until he should pay his debt. When his fellow servants saw what had happened, they were greatly distressed, and went to their master and laid the whole matter before him. So the master sent for the servant, and said to him 'You wicked servant! When you begged me for mercy, I forgave you the whole of that debt. Shouldn't you, also, to have shown mercy to your fellow servant, just as I showed mercy to you? Then his master, in anger, handed him over to the jailers, until he should pay the whole of his debt.

Matthew 20, 1-15
For the kingdom of heaven is like an employer who went out in the early morning to hire labourers for his vineyards. He agreed with the labourers to pay them the standard daily rate of two silver coins, and sent them into his vineyard. On going out again, about nine o'clock, he saw some others standing in the marketplace, doing nothing. 'You also may go into my vineyard,' he said, 'and I will pay you what is fair.' So they went. Going out again about midday and about three o'clock, he did as before. When he went out about five, he

found some others standing there, and said to them 'Why have you been standing here all day long, doing nothing?' 'Because no one has hired us,' they answered. 'You also may go into my vineyard,' he said. In the evening the owner of the vineyard said to his steward 'Call the labourers, and pay them their wages, beginning with the last, and ending with the first. Now when those who had been hired about five o'clock went up, they received two silver coins each. So, when the first went up, they thought that they would receive more, but they also received two silver coins each; on which they began to grumble at their employer. 'These last,' they said, 'have done only one hour's work, and yet you have put them on the same footing with us, who have borne the brunt of the day's work, and the heat.' 'My friend,' was his reply to one of them, 'I am not treating you unfairly. Didn't you agree with me for two silver coins? Take what belongs to you, and go. I choose to give to this last man the same as to you. Have not I the right to do as I choose with what is mine? Are you envious because I am liberal?'

Matthew 22, 2-13
The kingdom of heaven may be compared to a king who gave a banquet in honour of

his son's wedding. He sent his servants to call those who had been invited to the banquet, but they were unwilling to come. A second time he sent some servants, with orders to say to those who had been invited 'I have prepared my breakfast, my cattle and fat beasts are killed and everything is ready; come to the banquet.' They, however, took no notice, but went off, one to their farm, another to their business; while the rest, seizing his servants, ill-treated them and killed them. The king, in anger, sent his troops, put those murderers to death, and set their city on fire. Then he said to his servants 'The banquet is prepared, but those who were invited were not worthy. So go to the cross-roads, and invite everyone you find to the banquet.' The servants went out into the roads and collected all the people whom they found, whether bad or good; and the bridal-hall was filled with guests. But, when the king went in to see his guests, he noticed there a man who had not put on a wedding-robe. So he said to him 'My friend, how is it that you came in here without a wedding-robe?' The man was speechless. Then the king said to the attendants 'Tie him hand and foot, and 'put him out into the darkness' outside, where there will be weeping and grinding of teeth.'

Mark 4, 26-32

This is what the kingdom of God is like — like a man who has scattered seed on the ground, and then sleeps by night and rises by day, while the seed is shooting up and growing — he knows not how. The ground bears the crop of itself — first the blade, then the ear, and then the full grain in the ear; but, as soon as the crop is ready, immediately he 'puts in the sickle because harvest has come'. To what can we liken the kingdom of God? By what can we illustrate it? Perhaps by the growth of a mustard seed. This seed, when sown in the ground, though it is smaller than all other seeds, yet, when sown, shoots up, and becomes larger than any other herb, and puts out great branches, so that even 'the wild birds can roost in its shelter.'

Luke 13, 18-21

What is the kingdom of God like? And to what can I liken it? It is like a mustard seed which a man took and put in his garden. The seed grew and became a tree, and the wild birds roosted in its branches. To what can I liken the kingdom of God? It is like some yeast which a woman took and covered in three pecks of flour, until the whole had risen.

Luke 13, 24
Strive to go in by the small door. Many, I tell you, will seek to go in, but they will not be able,

Luke 14, 16-23
A man was once giving a great dinner. He invited many people, and sent his servant, when it was time for the dinner, to say to those who had been invited 'Come, for everything is now ready.' They all with one accord began to ask to be excused. The first said to the servant 'I have bought a field and am obliged to go and look at it. I must ask you to consider me excused.' The next said 'I have bought five pairs of bullocks, and I am on my way to try them. I must ask you to consider me excused'; while the next said 'I am just married, and for that reason I am unable to come.' On his return the servant told his master all these answers. Then in anger the owner of the house said to his servant 'Go out at once into the streets and alleys of the town, and bring in here the poor, and the crippled, and the blind, and the lame.' Presently the servant said 'Sir, your order has been carried out, and still there is room. Go out,' the master said, 'into the roads and

hedgerows, and make people come in, so that my house may be filled;

Luke 17, 20-21
The kingdom of God does not come in a way that can be seen, nor will people say 'Look, here it is!' or 'There it is!' for the kingdom of God is within you!

Thomas 20, 2-4
It is like a mustard seed. It is the smallest of all seeds. But when it falls on tilled soil, it produces a great plant and becomes a shelter for birds of the sky.

Thomas 76, 1-2
The kingdom of the father is like a merchant who had a consignment of merchandise and who discovered a pearl. That merchant was shrewd. He sold the merchandise and bought the pearl alone for himself.

Thomas 96, 1-2
The kingdom of the father is like a certain woman. She took a little leaven, concealed it in some dough, and made it into large loaves.

Thomas 97, 1-4
The kingdom of the father is like a certain woman who was carrying a jar full of meal.

While she was walking on the road, still some distance from home, the handle of the jar broke and the meal emptied out behind her on the road. She did not realize it; she had noticed no accident. When she reached her house, she set the jar down and found it empty.

Thomas 98, 1-3
The kingdom of the father is like a certain man who wanted to kill a powerful man. In his own house he drew his sword and stuck it into the wall in order to find out whether his hand could carry through. Then he slew the powerful man.

Thomas 109, 1-3
The kingdom is like a man who had a hidden treasure in his field without knowing it. And after he died, he left it to his son. The son did not know (about the treasure). He inherited the field and sold it. And the one who bought it went plowing and found the treasure. He began to lend money at interest to whomever he wished.

Thomas 113, 2-4
It will not come by waiting for it. It will not be a matter of saying 'here it is' or 'there it is.' Rather, the kingdom of the father is spread out upon the earth, and men do not see it.

Jesus was very intent on making people understand what the Kingdom of God/Heaven was all about, exhibiting a great deal of patience and understanding for those struggling with overwhelming questions.

Living Your Faith

Jesus apparently had little to say about living your faith, which is not at all surprising because the life he led was true to his own faith and was an example to us all. He expected his followers to put everything on the line as he was doing. The fact that this saying has been repeated so often in the Gospels stresses the importance it carried for followers of The Way, people who were prepared to sacrifice everything including their lives because of their faith.

Matthew 5, 15
People do not light a lamp and put it under a basket, but on the lamp-stand, where it gives light to everyone in the house.

Mark 4, 21
Is a lamp brought to be put under a basket or under the couch, instead of being put on the lamp-stand?

Luke 8, 16

No one sets light to a lamp and then covers it with a bowl or puts it underneath a couch, but they put it on a lamp-stand, so that anyone who comes in may see the light.

Luke 11, 33

No one sets light to a lamp, and then puts it in the cellar or under a basket, but he puts it on the lamp-stand, so that anyone who comes in may see the light.

Thomas 33, 2-3

For no one lights a lamp and puts it under a bushel, nor does he put it in a hidden place, but rather he sets it on a lampstand so that everyone who enters and leaves will see its light.

Love

Over the centuries Christianity developed a mystique about Christian love, and yet Jesus appeared to say very little about it. The final quotation from Luke seems to equate love with self interest, but I expect the word 'respect' often could suitably be used in place of the word 'love'.

Matthew 5, 44

love your enemies,

Luke 6, 27
love your enemies,

Matthew 5, 46
For if you love only those who love you, what reward will you have? Even the tax-gatherers do this!

Luke 6, 32, 35
If you love only those who love you, what thanks will be due to you? Why, even the outcast love those who love them! But love your enemies,

Luke 6, 41-42
There were two people who were in debt to a moneylender; one owed five hundred silver coins, and the other fifty. As they were unable to pay, he forgave them both. Which of them, do you think, will love him the   *more?*

Mysteries Revealed

There are two fundamental messages in these words of Jesus, everything will be revealed but it is up to the individual to take the initiative and search for the revelation of the truth. These are very empowering concepts for the individual Christian, a promise that we can find the truth if we diligently search for it. It is easy to extend that beyond pouring over the written Gospels and suggest that it includes a great deal of soul searching, interaction with like minded people and living a life that is in concert with the teachings of Jesus.

Matthew 7, 7-8
Ask, and it will be given to you; search, and you will find; knock, and the door will be opened to you. For the person who asks receives, the person who searches finds, and to the door will be opened to the person who knocks.

Matthew 10, 26
There is nothing concealed which will not be revealed, nor anything hidden which will not become known.

Luke 8, 17
Nothing is hidden which will not be brought into the light of day, not ever kept hidden which will not someday become known and come into the light of day.

Luke 11, 9-10
And so I say to you — Ask, and your prayer will be granted: search, and you will find; knock, and the door will be opened to you.

For the person who asks receives, everyone who searches finds, and to the person who knocks the door will be opened.

Luke 12, 2
There is nothing, however covered up, which will not be uncovered, nor anything kept secret which will not become known.

Thomas 2, 1
Let him who seeks continue seeking until he finds.

Thomas 5, 2
For there is nothing hidden which will not become manifest.

Thomas 94, 1-2
He who seeks will find, and he who knocks will be let in.

No Home

This appears to be a rather self serving statement by Jesus to reaffirm his role as the Messiah because it fulfils a prophecy contained in the Hebrew Scriptures, but of course it is also true because Jesus had chosen to lead an itinerant life, which meant that he had no home.

Matthew 8, 20
Foxes have holes and wild birds their nests, but the Son of Man has nowhere to lay his head.

Luke 9, 58
Foxes have holes and wild birds their nests, but the Son of Man has nowhere to lay his head.

Thomas 86, 1-2
The foxes have their holes and the birds have their nests, but the son of man has no place to lay his head and rest.

No Respect At Home

Like the earlier entry with respect to 'No Home' this clearly connects Jesus with the prophetic reference in the Judaic Scriptures that helps confirm his position as the Messiah.

Matthew 13, 57
A prophet is not without honour, except in his own country and in his own house.

Mark 6, 4
A prophet is not without honour, except in his own country, and among his own relations, and in his own home.

Luke 4, 24
I tell you that no prophet is acceptable in his own country.

John 4, 44
a prophet is not honoured in his own country.

Thomas 31, 1
No prophet is accepted in his own village.

Good Gifts

Matthew 7, 9-11
Who among you, when their child asks them for bread, will give them a stone, or when they ask for a fish, will give them a snake? If you, then, wicked though you are, know how to give good gifts to your children, how much more will your Father who is in heaven give what is good to those who ask him!

Powerful Man

These are very strange words when viewed without any contextual setting, but unfortunately that is all we have. For a culture that has as one of its earliest commandments 'you should not steal', it seems strange to use an analogy of plundering, although the truthfulness of the statements are incontestable.

Matthew 12, 29
How, again, can anyone get into a strong man's house and carry off his goods, without first securing him? Not until then will he plunder his house.

Mark 3, 27
No man who has got into a strong man's house can carry off his goods, without first securing him; and not until then will he plunder his house.

Luke 11, 21-22
When a strong man is keeping guard, fully armed, over his own mansion, his property is in safety; but, when one still stronger has attacked and overpowered him, he takes away all the weapons on which the other had relied, and divides his spoil.

Thomas 35, 1-2
It is not possible for anyone to enter the house of a strong man and take it by force unless he binds his hands; then he will be able to ransack his house.

Salting the Salt

Salt was a very expensive commodity in the developing world of the first century, providing a perfect backdrop for Jesus to demonstrate the difference between cost in the secular world and value to God.

Matthew 5, 13
You are salt for the world. But if salt becomes tasteless, how can it be made salty again? It is no longer good for anything, but is thrown away, and trampled underfoot.

Mark 9, 50
Salt is good, but, if the salt should lose its saltiness, what will you use to season it?

Luke 14, 34-35
Yes, salt is good; but, if the salt itself should lose its strength, what will be used to season it? It is not fit either for the land or for the manure heap. People throw it away.

Old Wine-skins

Mark 2, 22
And no one ever puts new wine into old wine-skins; if they do, the wine will burst the

*skins, and both the wine and the skins are
lost. But new wine is put into fresh skins.*

Luke 5, 37-38
*And no one puts new wine into old wine-
skins; for, if they do, the new wine will burst
the skins, and the wine itself will run out,
and the skins be lost. But new wine must be
put into fresh skins.*

Thomas 47, 4
*And new wine is not put into old wineskins,
lest they burst; nor is old wine put into a
new wineskin, lest it spoil it.*

Fasting and Wedding

This saying is a clear reference to Jesus
and the future, with Jesus as the groom.
Jesus knows his days are numbered
because that is the prophecy that he is
fulfilling, and he is laying the groundwork for
his followers to understand that the Old
Testament prophecies relate directly to him.

Matthew 9, 15
*Can the groom's friends mourn as long as
the groom is with them? But the days will
come, when the groom will be taken away
from them, and they will fast then.*

Mark 2, 19
Can the groom's friends fast, while the groom is with them? As long as they have the groom with them, they cannot fast.

Luke 5, 34
Can you make the groom's friends fast while the groom is with them?

Children

Much has been made of these passages over the centuries to encourage people to be childlike and accept what they have been told. That is not what Jesus meant at all, the image of the sheep blindly following the shepherd is a construct of the post first century church as a means to manipulate and control the population. In this passage Jesus meant that a person who examines their soul and comes to a clear understanding of their relationship with God will lose their worldliness and become childlike in their innocence and faith.

Matthew 19, 14
Haven't you read that at the beginning the Creator 'made them male and female,'

Mark 10, 14b

Let the little children come to me, do not hinder them; for it is to the childlike that the kingdom of God belongs.

Luke 18, 16
Let the little children come to me, and do not hinder them; for it is to the childlike that the kingdom of God belongs.

Able-Bodied and Sick

Matthew 9, 12
It is not those who are healthy who need a doctor, but those who are ill.

Mark 2, 17a
It is not those who are healthy who need a doctor, but those who are ill.

Luke 5, 31
It is not those who are well who need a doctor, but those who are ill.

By Their Fruit They Are Known

Matthew 7, 16
Do people pick grapes from thorn bushes, or figs from thistles?

Thomas 45, 1

Grapes are not harvested from thorns, nor are figs gathered from thistles, for they do not produce fruit.

Aged Wine

Luke 5, 39
No one after drinking old wine wishes for new.

Thomas 47, 3
No man drinks old wine and immediately desires to drink new wine.

Mountain City

Matthew 5, 14
A town that stands on a hill cannot be hidden.

Thomas 32
A city being built on a high mountain and fortified cannot fall, nor can it be hidden.

God and Sparrows

These are simplistic words designed to give people comfort in the same way that the Beatitudes were delivered. Jesus was speaking to a particular audience who needed this level of assurance, demonstrating his ability to relate to people at all levels.

Luke, 12, 6-7
Are not five sparrows sold for two copper coins? Yet not one of them has escaped God's notice. No, even the hairs of your head are all numbered. Do not be afraid; you are of more value than many sparrows.

Matthew 10, 29-31
Are not two sparrows sold for a one copper coin? Yet not one of them will fall to the ground without your Father's knowledge. While as for you, even the hairs of your head are numbered. Do not, therefore, be afraid; you are of more value than many sparrows.

Barren Tree

Luke 13, 6-9
A man, who had a fig tree growing in his vineyard, came to look for fruit on it, but could not find any. So he said to his gardener 'Three years now I have come to look for fruit on this fig tree, without finding any! Cut it down. Why should it rob the soil?' 'Leave it this one year more, Sir,' the man answered, 'until I have dug around it and manured it. Then, if it bears in future,

well and good; but if not, you can have it cut down.'

Return of Evil Spirit

These words speak to the futility of purging oneself of evil practices without filling the vessel with something good. It is not enough to be without evil and empty, but we must fill that void with the glory of God.

Luke 11, 24-26
No sooner does a foul spirit leave someone, than it passes through places where there is no water, in search of rest; and finding none, it says 'I will go back to the home which I left'; but, on coming there, it finds it unoccupied, swept, and put in order. Then it goes and brings with it seven other spirits more wicked than itself, and they go in, and make their home there; and the last state of that person proves to be worse than the first.

Fire on Earth

This is a wonderful saying that by itself was a prophecy that has come true, Jesus lit the fire and eventually it engulfed the known world. The absence of this saying in the synoptic Gospels is surprising, it is found only in the Gospel of Thomas.

Thomas 10
I have cast fire upon the world, and see, I am guarding it until it blazes.

Inside and Outside

Thomas 89, 1-2
Why do you wash the outside of the cup? Do you not realize that he who made the inside is the same one who made the outside?

Nature of God

Matthew 5, 45
for he causes his sun to rise on bad and good alike, and sends rain on the righteous and on the unrighteous.

First and Last

Matthew 20, 16
So those who are last will be first, and the first last.

Our Anxieties

People are people no matter where or when they live. The anxieties that people felt in 30 CE are very like those that people feel today, and these words of advice are just as relevant today as they were then.

Matthew 6, 25-30
This is why I say to you: Do not be anxious about your life — what you can get to eat or drink, or about your body — what you can get to wear. Is not life more than food, and the body more than clothing? Look at the wild birds — they neither sow, nor reap, nor gather into barns; and yet your heavenly Father feeds them! Aren't you more precious than they? But which of you, by being anxious, can prolong their life a single moment? And why be anxious about clothing? Study the wild lilies, and how they grow. They neither toil nor spin; yet I tell you that even Solomon in all his splendor was not robed like one of these. If God so clothes even the grass of the field, which is living today and tomorrow will be thrown into the oven, will not he much more clothe you, you of little faith?

Luke 12, 22-25
That is why I say to you, do not be anxious about the life here — what you can get to eat; or about your body — what you can get

to wear. For life is more than food, and the body than its clothes. Think of the ravens — they neither sow nor reap; they have neither storehouse nor barn; and yet God feeds them! And how much more precious are you than birds! But which of you, by being anxious, can prolong your life a moment?

Luke 12, 27-28
Think of the lilies, and how they grow. They neither toil nor spin; yet, I tell you, even Solomon in all his splendor was not robed like one of these. If, even in the field, God so clothes the grass which is living today and tomorrow will be thrown into the oven, how much more will he clothe you, you of little faith!

Thomas 36, 2
Do not be concerned from morning until evening and from evening until morning about what you will wear.

Persistence

Jesus clearly encouraged persistence and tenacity in his followers, otherwise the Jesus Movement would not have survived more than a couple of generations following his death. Being persistent was an undercurrent of everything he did, so perhaps it is not surprising that there are few words existing that directly relate to it.

Luke 11, 5-8
Suppose that one of you who has a friend were to go to him in the middle of the night and say 'Friend, lend me three loaves, for a friend of mine has arrived at my house after a journey, and I have nothing to offer him;' And suppose that the other should answer from inside 'Do not trouble me; the door is already fastened, and my children and I are in bed; I cannot get up and give you anything'; I tell you that, even though he will not get up and give him anything because he is a friend, yet because of his persistence he will rouse himself and give him what he wants.

Luke 18, 2-5
There was in a certain town a judge, who had no fear of God nor regard for people. In the same town there was a widow who went to him again and again, and said 'Grant me justice against my opponent.' For a time the judge refused, but afterwards he said to himself 'Although I am without fear of God or regard for people, 5 yet, as this widow is so troublesome, I will grant her

justice, to stop her from plaguing me with her endless visits.'

Prayer

Prayer is a fundamental part of the Judaic faith and the followers of Jesus did not need instruction in the basic approach, but he did see fit to fine tune things a little so they were synchronic with his overall message. It is an intensely Jewish form of prayer that is totally in harmony with the times and environment of first century Judea. Over time additional words were added and it became known as the Lord's Prayer, a basic functional piece that is widely used in every Christian gathering.

These additions, all of which were made in the second and third centuries, clearly illustrate the editorial license taken by the early church leadership as it sought to influence the minds of its congregants. Compare the Lord's Prayer as you recite it in your own church with the following passages and you will get some idea of the extent of revisionism that was applied.

Matthew 6, 9, 11 – 12
Our Father, may your name be held holy,
 your kingdom come,

103

Give us today the bread that we will need;
and forgive us our wrong-doings,
as we have forgiven those who have
wronged us;

Luke 11, 2
Father,
May your name be held holy,
your kingdom come.

Humility before God is the message in this parable about prayer. The closing line in this saying parallels the message contained in Matthew 20,16, that the last shall be first and the first shall be last.

Luke 18, 10-14
Two men went up into the Temple Courts to pray. One was a Pharisee and the other a tax gatherer. The Pharisee stood forward and began praying to himself in this way — 'God, I thank you that I am not like other men — thieves, rogues, adulterers — or even like this tax gatherer. I fast twice a week, and give a tenth of everything I get to God.' Meanwhile the tax gatherer stood at a distance, not venturing even 'to raise his eyes to heaven'; but he kept striking his breast and saying 'God, have mercy on me, a sinner.' This man, I tell you, went home pardoned, rather than the other; for

everyone who exalts himself will be humbled, while everyone who humbles himself will be exalted.

Rejoice! The Lost Is Found

This is a clear reference to redemption in the eyes of God, one that we all find acceptable until we run into the problems that are created by the Parable of the Lost Son. Those of us who aspire to live a life of humility, while trying to walk in the path that Jesus taught, can all relate to the feeling of the brother who never left, that just was not fair! No it was not fair, but it is consistent with the message that Jesus taught about the last will be first and those who want to be first will be last, and riches in this world do not matter in the greater scheme of things.

Matthew 18, 12-13
What think you? If a person owns a hundred sheep, and one of them strays, will the person not leave the ninety-nine on the hills, and go and search for the one that is straying? And, if they succeed in finding it, I tell you that they rejoice more over that one sheep than over the ninety-nine which did not stray.

Luke 15, 4-6

Who among you who has a hundred sheep, and has lost one of them, does not leave the ninety-nine out in the open country, and go after the lost sheep until he finds it? And, when he has found it, he puts in on his shoulders rejoicing; and, on reaching home, he calls his friends and his neighbours together, and says 'Come and rejoice with me, for I have found my sheep which was lost.'

Luke 15, 8-9

Or again, what woman who has ten silver coins, if she loses one of them, does not light a lamp, and sweep the house, and search carefully until she finds it? And, when she has found it, she calls her friends and neighbours together, and says 'Come and rejoice with me, for I have found the coin which I lost.'

Luke 15, 11-32

A man had two sons and the younger of them said to his father 'Father, give me my share of the inheritance.' So the father divided the property between them. A few days later the younger son got together all that he had, and went away into a distant land; and there he squandered his inheritance by leading a dissolute life. After he has spent all that he had, there was a severe famine through all that country, and he began to be in actual want. So he went and engaged himself to one of the people of that country, who sent him into his fields to tend pigs. He even longed to satisfy his hunger with the bean-pods on which the pigs were feeding; and no one gave him anything. But, when he came to himself, he said 'How many of my father's hired servants have more bread than they can eat, while here am I starving to death! I will get up and go to my father, and say to him "Father, I sinned against heaven and against you; I am no longer fit to be called your son; make me one of your hired servants." And he got up and went to his father. But, while he was still a long way off, his father saw him and was deeply moved; he ran and threw his arms around his neck and kissed him. 'Father,' the son said, 'I sinned against heaven and against you; I am no longer fit to be called your son; make me one of your hired servants.' But the father turned to his servants and said 'Be quick and fetch a robe — the very best — and put it on him; give him a ring for his finger and sandals for his feet; and bring the fattened calf and kill it, and let us eat and make merry; for here is my son who was dead, and is alive again, was lost, and is found.' So they began making merry. Meanwhile the elder son was out in the fields; but, on coming home, when he got near the house, he heard music and dancing, and he called one of the servants and asked what it all meant. 'Your brother has come back,' the servant told him, 'and your father has killed the fattened calf, because he has him back safe and sound.' This made him angry, and he would not go in. But his father came out and begged him to do so. 'No,' he said to his father, 'look at all the years I have been serving you, without ever once disobeying you, and yet you have never given me even a young goat, so that I might have a merrymaking with my friends. But, no sooner has this son of yours come, who has eaten up your property in the company of prostitutes, then you have killed the fattened calf for him.' 'Child,' the father answered, 'you are always with me, and everything that I have is yours. We could but make merry and rejoice, for here is your brother who was dead, and is alive; who was lost, and is found.'

Rich Persons Conundrum

The Middle East was really no different in 30 CE from the modern world in at least one respect, power and money were intrinsically connected and jealously controlled by a minority of the population. Jesus came from the other side of the tracks, he was a landless peasant who relied on daily work to sustain himself and his family, and was now in the process of building a following amongst the common people. Exploitation by the rich has been a recurring reality throughout history and the quickest way to garner support among the 99% who are disenfranchised was to attack the rich and powerful.

This created a real conflict for Jesus because he knew that he had to gain recognition by those in positions of authority, and draw enough of them to his cause, to give it the momentum that it needed. In hindsight he was successful, if not directly then through his followers who carried Christianity through the first century. How did Jesus overcome this and get invited into the homes of the rich? It must have required a healthy dose of tenacity and a message that resonated with people of conscience who just happened to be rich. Is it much of a stretch to suggest that Jesus may have been very politically astute? It is fundamentally no different today, although in our Western society the extremes of rich and poor do not marginalize large numbers of people to the point where they live from day to day, unlike in the Third World where the situation is a much greater parallel with the first century reality.

So what is a rich person to do? Not too many of us who call ourselves Christian would be inclined to accept the advice Jesus gives as recorded in Mark 10, 20: *go and sell all that you have and give to the poor and then come and follow me.* This advice is contrary to that given in the parables about stewardship, society through the ages has always opted for the solid stewardship of assets over extreme acts of charity as counselled by Jesus, and will perpetually continue to do so.

It would appear that Jesus fell into the same trap that exists for all of us, we need money to survive so we all need to find a balance between meeting our primary needs and Christian charity. How did Jesus do this? Probably the same way most practising Christians manage to get around the problem, negotiating a compromise within ourselves, accentuating the positive and minimizing the negative aspects of this message.

It appears that many of the initial recruits did just that however, and the early community structure adopted by followers of The Way was clearly one of communal sharing. In the book of Acts which was written by Luke, this is discussed in considerable detail. The apostle Peter deliberately killed a couple who falsely claimed to have contributed all their wealth to the community pool while withholding half of it. It is remarkable how quickly the emerging Christian hierarchy chose to downplay this foundational piece as it developed its own base of power and wealth. The communal policy was found to be unworkable and thereafter was reserved for smaller religious communities which are today known as monastic orders.

Matthew 6, 24
No one can serve two masters, for either they will hate one and love the other, or else they will attach themselves to one and despise the other. You cannot serve both God and Money.

Matthew 19, 23-24
I tell you that a rich person will find it hard to enter the kingdom of heaven! I say again, it is easier for a camel to get through a

needle's eye than for a rich person to enter the kingdom of heaven!

Mark 10, 20
There is still one thing wanting in you; go and sell all that you have, and give to the poor, and you will have wealth in heaven; then come and follow me.

Mark 10, 25
It is easier for a camel to get through a needle's eye, than for a rich person to enter the kingdom of God.

Luke 12, 16-20
There was once a rich man whose land was very fertile; and he began to ask himself 'What will I do, for I have nowhere to store my crops? This is what I will do,' he said; 'I will pull down my barns and build larger ones, and store all my grain and my goods in them; and I will say to myself, now you have plenty of good things put by for many years; take your ease, eat, drink, and enjoy yourself.' But God said to the man 'Fool! This very night your life is being demanded; and as for all you have prepared — who will have it?'

Luke 16, 13

No servant can serve two masters, for, either they will hate one and love the other, or else they will attach themselves to one and despise the other. You cannot serve both God and Money.

Luke 18, 25
It is easier, indeed, for a camel to get through a needle's eye than for a rich person to enter the kingdom of God!

Thomas 47, 2
And it is impossible for a servant to serve two masters; otherwise, he will honour the one and treat the other contemptuously.

Thomas 63, 1-6
There was a rich man who had much money. He said, 'I shall put my money to use so that I may sow, reap, plant, and fill my storehouse with produce, with the result that I shall lack nothing.' Such were his intentions, but that same night he died. Let him who has ears hear.

Satan

The existence of evil, the dark side of our existence, has been acknowledged in all cultures since the beginning of time. Just as societies tried to capture God in a picture, as Michelangelo did in the Sistine Chapel, they tried to depict evil as a bizarre and odious caricature; hence the drawings of the devil as a fiendish goat or flame belching dragon. Various names were also developed as synonyms for evil, and it is important to remember that the personification of evil by using names like Beelzebub and Satan does not diminish its insidious power to destroy. Evil, like the power of God, can be visible and invisible.

Gehenna is generally equated to hell, but it is a word that had an interesting evolution into the notion of hell that is embraced today in virtually every Christian denomination. Gehenna was the garbage dump outside the walls of Jerusalem that took everything from everyday trash to animal carcasses and unclaimed cadavers, where fires burned night and day to reduce the stench of decay. Gehenna was a real place in first century Judea, a place that was known by everyone and avoided as much as possible. It was quite literally an example of hell on earth and the church fathers wasted no time in developing an appropriate mythology.

Matthew 12, 27-28

And, if it is by Beelzebub's help that I drive out demons, by whose help is it that your own sons drive them out? Therefore they will themselves be your judges. But, if it is by the help of the Spirit of God that I drive out demons, then the kingdom of God must already be upon you.

Luke 10, 18
I have had visions of Satan, fallen, like lightning from the heavens.

Luke 11, 17-20
Any kingdom wholly divided against itself becomes a desolation; and a divided house falls. So, too, if Satan is wholly divided against himself, how can his kingdom last? Yet you say that I drive out demons by the help of Beelzebub. But, if it is by Beelzebub's help that I drive out demons, by whose help is it that your own sons drive them out? Therefore they will themselves be your judges. But, if it is by the hand of God that I drive out demons, then the kingdom of God must already be upon you.

Son of Man/Son of God

In the Old Testament the term Son of Man was used by prophets to signify to their followers that they were not the promised

Messiah, they were of human rather than godly origin. When Jesus first began to use this term to describe himself it was a wilful act to identify himself as an extension of the Old Testament prophets. This served his interests in two ways, it automatically built a historical bridge with popular prophets and, by extension, established a very special relationship with God that set him apart from all the other prophets of his time. It also underscored the fact that Jesus was not to be represented as a warrior Messiah. Look at the words Jesus spoke at the time of his baptism by John the Baptist.

John the Baptist was a figure in history, and his entrance into the Gospel writings really marks the end of the fictional histories of Jesus, and became a factually based rendering of his story. Both Matthew and Luke have created a plausible scenario in which they were able to set these words of Jesus, and a reading of the full passage in both Gospels is recommended. The Pharisees are out to watch John and see if he violated any of the Temple laws, these were taunting words addressed by Jesus to the Pharisees.

Matthew 11, 8
What did you go out into the wilderness to look at? A reed waving in the wind? If not,

what did you go out to see? A man richly dressed? Why, those who wear rich things are to be found in the courts of kings!

Luke 7, 25
What did you go out into the wilderness to look at? A reed and waving in the wind? If not, what did you go out to see? A man dressed in rich clothing? Why, those who are accustomed to fine clothes and luxury live in royal palaces.

Thomas 78, 1-2
Why have you come out into the desert? To see a reed shaken by the wind?

If these words had been chosen to kick start Jesus' ministry they certainly succeeded. He immediately drew attention to himself for the benefit of the crowd, who would have been shocked by his speaking to the Pharisees in such a manner. The Pharisees expected subservience from their lessers, and the insults received by the Pharisees would be reported in great detail back at the Temple. This sets the scene for a carefully orchestrated three year journey that would see many of the ancient prophecies fulfilled.

Let us for a moment consider the other possibilities available to Jesus. If he had come out swinging, claiming to be the Messiah and the Son of God as he strolled up the hill from the River Jordan, the general population would have acclaimed him as the new general that would drive the Romans away, and the Romans would have ended his career very quickly. The Pharisees would have been quick to accuse him of blasphemy which was punishable by death, but capital punishment was only available to the Romans so the Temple court would have gladly handed him over. But that was not to be, Jesus pursued a very well planned strategy to fulfil the prophecies while allowing his followers to make the claims of his divinity, which Jesus did not deny.

The Hebrew Scriptures as they exist today were finalized in the first century BCE. These were the scriptures that Jesus would have studied as a child, they are the scriptures that he referred to during his mission. They regularly use the term Son of Man in the context that describes a human being as distinct from the hoped for Messiah, who would be the Son of God. The prophets all took great care to identify themselves as Sons of Man to reinforce their humanness to their followers, and that is how Jesus began his ministry. During his ministry his followers started questioning whether he was in fact the Son of God and Jesus never denied it, although he never came out and blatantly affirmed that he was the chosen one. As a result, the meaning of the two terms became blurred and were used interchangeably by the time of the crucifixion and resurrection

This appears to be part of the grand design for fulfilling scriptural prophecy used by Jesus for his ministry, his followers were only too quick to oblige because, as the importance of Jesus grew, his followers became part of a select group. Making these two terms synonymous was instituted by Jesus, constantly referring to himself as the Son of Man while encouraging his followers to think Son of God. It was very easy for his flock to posthumously, in fact within a matter of days, decide that he was the Son of God.

As evidence to support these conclusions I offer you a parable contained only in the book of Thomas, the only surviving writings from one of the disciples. The parable was to be interpreted that God owned the earth and gave it to his people, he sent a series of prophets and finally sent his son Jesus who was killed. This parable is a perfect example of the way in which Jesus demonstrated to his followers that he was

119

the Son of God without blatantly saying it. *"Let him who has ears hear."*

Thomas 65, 1-7
There was a good man who owned a vineyard. He leased it to tenant farmers so that they might work it and he might collect the produce from them. He sent his servant so that the tenants might give him the produce of the vineyard. They seized his servant and beat him, all but killing him. The servant went back and told his master. The master said, 'Perhaps he did not recognize them.' He sent another servant. The tenants beat this one as well. Then the owner sent his son and said, 'Perhaps they will show respect to my son.' Because the tenants knew that it was he who was the heir to the vineyard, they seized him and killed him. Let him who has ears hear.

There are many references to Son of Man in the sayings contained in this book, generally they were used by Jesus to identify himself, thereby emphasizing that he only ever claimed that he was a man of the people.

Luke 6, 34
and now that the Son of Man has come, eating and drinking, you are saying 'Here is

a glutton and a wine-drinker, a friend of tax-
gatherers and outcasts.

Stewardship

These parables about stewardship are very
complex in that they deal with the
obligations of stewardship and, in the piece
from Luke, appears to place honesty below
the need to satisfy the expectations of the
employer. Does Jesus really mean that the
end justifies the means? It reinforces the
view that he was a pragmatic man with a
mission, and it seems likely that he did not
disapprove of manipulative conduct that
satisfied the objective.

Matthew 25, 14-28
For it is as though a man, going on his
travels, called his servants, and gave his
property into their charge. He gave five
bags of gold to one, two to another, and
one bag to a third, in proportion to the
ability of each. Then he set out on his
travels. The servant who had received the
five bags of gold went at once and traded
with it, and made another five bags. So,
too, the servant who had received the two
bags of gold made another two bags. But
the servant who had received the one bag
went and dug a hole in the ground, and hid

his master's money. After a long time the master of those servants returned, and settled accounts with them. The servant who had received the five bags of gold came up and brought five bags more. 'Sir,' he said, 'you entrusted me with five bags of gold; look, I have made another five bags!' 'Well done, good, trustworthy servant!' said his master. 'You have been trustworthy with a small sum; now I will place a large one in your hands; come and share your master's joy!' Then the one who had received the two bags of gold came up and said 'Sir, you entrusted me with two bags pounds; look, I have made another two!' 'Well done, good, trustworthy servant!' said his master. 'You have been trustworthy with a small sum; now I will place a large one in your hands; come and share your master's joy!' The man who had received the single bag of gold came up, too, and said 'Sir, I knew that you were a hard man; you reap where you have not sown, and gather up where you have not winnowed; and, in my fear, I went and hid your money in the ground; look, here is what belongs to you!' 'You lazy, worthless servant!' was his master's reply. 'You knew that I reap where I have not sown, and gather up where I have not winnowed? Then you ought to have placed my money in the hands of bankers, and I, on my return, should have received my money, with interest. 'Therefore,' he continued, 'take away from him the one bag of gold, and give it to the one who has the ten bags.'

Luke 16, 1-8

There was a rich man who had a steward; and this steward was maliciously accused to him of wasting his estate. So the master called him and said 'What is this that I hear about you? Give in your accounts, for you cannot act as steward any longer.' 'What am I to do,' the steward asked himself, 'now that my master is taking the steward's place away from me? I have not strength to dig, and I am ashamed to beg. I know what I will do, so that, as soon as I am turned out of my stewardship, people may welcome me into their homes.' One by one he called up his master's debtors. 'How much do you owe my master?' he asked of the first. Four hundred and forty gallons of oil,' answered the man. 'Here is your agreement,' he said; 'sit down at once and make it two hundred and twenty.' And you, the steward said to the next, 'how much do you owe?' 'Seventy quarters of wheat,' he replied. 'Here is your agreement,' the steward said; 'make it fifty-six.' His master complimented this dishonest steward on the shrewdness of his action.

The Sabbath

One of the 10 Commandments delivered by Moses required that the seventh day be considered holy, and the Jewish faith honoured that tradition to a degree that most of us would consider a little extreme. Jesus clearly felt that way.

Mark 2, 27-28
The Sabbath was made for people, and not people for the Sabbath; so the Son of Man is lord even of the Sabbath.

Luke 6, 5
The Son of Man is lord even of the Sabbath.

Luke 13, 15-16
You hypocrites! Does not every one of you let your ox or your ass loose from its manger, and take it out to drink, on the Sabbath? But this woman, a daughter of Abraham, who has been kept in bondage by Satan for now eighteen years, ought not she to have been released from her bondage on the Sabbath?

3 - Actions Speak Louder ....

The primary sources for information about the actions that Jesus had taken as he pursued his ministry and mission are the Gospels of Mark, Matthew and Luke. The oral tradition would have kept these stories alive, and were readily available to the Gospel writers. Their authenticity is not in question, but for the purposes of our study their contents are of value to us as a suitable indication of what was believed by the first two generations following the crucifixion. Our goal is to understand why this new Judaic sect spread across the world like wildfire, therefore we must come to a firm understanding of what they believed to be true.

In spring the Judean hills come alive with promise as the sun warms the soil and everything comes to life. The rivers enjoy a regular flow that will last well into the middle of the summer when the streams will become a tinkling trickle over their rocky bottom. It is now late spring and the water in the Jordan River is a refreshing but tolerable temperature, ideal conditions for the baptisms that John is performing in the middle of the stream. Standing in waist deep water with his clothing tied up above the reach of the water, he greets each of the pilgrims as they drop their clothing on the riverbank and wade in to meet him.

Pulling an old man to his feet after his submersion John passed him to a helper who steadied him on the slippery rocks as he moved back to the shore. Turning towards the next candidate John thought there must be some mistake, why was Jesus here in the middle of the stream with him? When John protested that he should be baptized by Jesus, he was told that Jesus had to do everything that God required, which included baptism by John.

This encounter was a scriptural prophecy that was fulfilled, although it is very likely that Jesus, being aware of the prophecy, made sure it happened that way. This baptism also sent a very important message to the people that Jesus would be interacting with, he was not coming as a conquering king to whom John should be subservient, but he was coming as a normal person confessing his sins and being baptized just like every other pilgrim.

Jesus was profoundly affected by the baptism experience, following which he went into the wilderness to be alone for some time. It was the first step in a ministry that he knew would end with pain and suffering, and he needed time alone to commune with God, strengthen his will and address his personal demons. Every person carries their own demons deep within themselves and Jesus was no exception, we all have our individual demons that assail us. We have all experienced our own times in the wilderness where we have been tempted in different directions, arrived at conclusions and come back to society with a better understanding of our purpose, and the direction that our lives should take.

When Jesus returned from his self imposed exile he found that John had been arrested by the Temple guards. He then headed to Galilee and, according to Mark, was proclaiming that the kingdom of God was at hand, it was time to repent and believe the good news. Jesus was following in the footsteps of the prophets that had gone before, clearly establishing his credentials as a genuine prophet in the eyes of the Jewish people. At the same time, he was developing a cadre of followers, some of whom would have joined his company and traveled with him, although most of the people hearing his message would have been day trippers who heard that he was in the area, or casual observers in the marketplace or synagogue who returned home to talk of this new prophet who spoke with such authority.

As he was passing the Sea of Galilee Jesus started to recruit specific people to join his team. His message must have been incredibly powerful because these men left their families, their fishing boats and their nets behind. In the structure of extended families that existed throughout antiquity and into the 19th century CE, this abandonment was not nearly as devastating for families as it would be in modern times. Other members of the extended family would have picked up the nets, climbed in the boats and kept the family fed.

Jesus and his followers then went on to Capernaum where they visited the synagogue and Jesus began to teach, not only as an interpreter of the law in the manner that the Pharisees would do, but he spoke with great authority. When confronted by a man who was possessed Jesus exorcised the foul spirit, which of course had an immediate and profound impact on the members of the congregation, resulting in his fame spreading like wildfire. He subsequently cured Simon's mother in law of a fever, which simply enhanced his stature in the community. Word of Jesus' presence spread quickly and by nightfall crowds were clamouring to have their friends and relatives cured. When Jesus did so he counseled people not to speak of the cures, which of course was a surefire way to make sure the message spread even faster.

The pressure of the crowds continued, so the following morning Jesus decided to move on to other country towns where he could make his proclamation known to everyone. Speaking in the synagogues and to the crowds was important for Jesus because it gave him an opportunity to get his message out, but wherever he went he was surrounded by people looking for cures, which he happily provided. After he cured a leper the pressure became far too intense in the communities, so Jesus and his followers stayed outside towns in lonely places where people had to travel to see him.

Needless to say, word spread rapidly back to Jerusalem about what was happening in Galilee and the keepers of the law began to monitor everything that Jesus did, looking for opportunities to exert some scripturally based legal control over him. Jesus was having a seriously successful run at disrupting the Jewish establishment and this was not making the people in power very happy. The teachers of the law, who by this time were following Jesus everywhere, huddled to discuss what they should do about this blasphemer. Jesus called out to them and asked why they were debating this. He challenged them "which is easier? — to say to the paralyzed man, 'Your sins are forgiven'? Or to say 'Get up, and take up your mat, and walk'?" Jesus then turned to a paralyzed man in the crowd and cured him.

Jesus later recruited a tax collector, Matthew. The disciples and Jesus went to dinner at Matthew's house with a number of tax collectors and other social outcasts, many of whom were followers. Word of this got back to the Pharisees very quickly of course, by this time they were looking for every opportunity to discredit him. When Jesus heard of their complaint about him passing his time in the company of outcasts it gave him a perfect opening to both validate his work and put the Pharisees in a position where they would look foolish if they did not agree. His defence was simple, he had come to minister to the outcasts of the world, not the religious, so why should he be in the company of the overtly religious Pharisees? Just imagine the level of frustration this must have caused in the ranks of the Temple authorities!

The way the disciples lived was not fully consistent with conventional Jewish behaviour, although it certainly was not outside the law. They did not fast at the usual times nor did they follow many of the purifying rituals that are usual in their society, and they certainly did not care what others were thinking about them. According to Mark, this was when Jesus gave the prophetic parable about the groom's friends, asking if they can fast while the groom is with them? They cannot fast while the groom is with them, but when the groom is taken away they will have lots of time for fasting.

The nitpicking Pharisees were an easy target for a man with the intelligence and quick wit that Jesus had. The spies were active one Sabbath when the disciples were walking through a farmer's field, picking and eating food as they went. The Pharisees jumped on this because they were working (harvesting food) on the Sabbath, but Jesus predictably had an appropriate response at the ready; giving him the opportunity to claim the Sabbath was made for people, not people for the Sabbath.

Nevertheless, they continued to bait him. Jesus went to a synagogue for Sabbath services and there was a man there with a crippled hand. The setup was obvious to Jesus but he turned to the congregation and asked if it was allowable to do good on the Sabbath or harm? To save a life or destroy it? He then healed the crippled hand.

Jesus did not shy away from conflict, although he was very careful about how he rose to the challenge. We can all understand the anger he would feel at such hypocrisy, but the real lesson here is recognizing how he controlled his anger and channeled it in a very focused way to meet his objective. Once again the man Jesus shows us unequivocally that his actions are consistent with his words.

By now Jesus was being followed constantly, being hounded by the masses of people who craved his healing touch. They just wanted to be around him because he clearly was a messenger from God, unlike any they had ever seen. Not surprisingly, he was also followed by a fringe group that today we would refer to as fanatics or extremists, whereas Mark calls them foul spirits. These are the people that loudly proclaimed that Jesus was the Son of God, which of course was not something Jesus wanted to have broadcast at this point in his ministry, that would come in due course in accordance with his well planned strategy.

Recognizing that his growing popularity was making excessive demands on his time Jesus decided to develop some leverage by officially appointing his apostles, the 12 disciples. By this time, he had a significant cadre of committed disciples/followers, and the appointment of 12 people as insiders with direct access to Jesus was a very significant step. These disciples had a very specific role to play, they would remain close by him so he could send them out as his representatives to preach the good news. This first century structure for organizational management bears a striking similarity to what we find in the 21st century, which once again underscores that people from the earliest times to today are substantially the same.

All of those people who found Jesus an embarrassment or a thorn in their side very quickly tried to discount his credibility by calling him a madman. His relations came to collect him because they said he was out of his mind, the teachers of the law from Jerusalem said he was the tool of the devil, using some very circumspect logic to justify their claim. These misguided people still did not understand the incredible intellect of the man they tackled in a battle of wits, and Jesus proceeded to verbally crucify each and every argument that was raised. Eventually Jesus' relatives brought his immediate family to pressure him, which gave rise to the comments from Jesus about the very important distinction between our birth family and our adult family of likeminded people. How many times have we heard people remark that you cannot choose your family of birth, but fortunately you can choose your family of friends?

Teaching by the sea had its advantages, when the crowds grew too large and were pressing on all sides Jesus could climb in a boat and get a little personal space. This is easy to visualize, is it not? The teacher sitting at ease in a fishing boat or skiff on this freshwater lake, while the hills leading down to the water are full of people sitting on the grass and listening intently. Jesus delivered many parables in this kind of setting, always on his guard about making claims that could be used against him because the Pharisees always had their spies in the crowds.

Parables are stories that have a hidden meaning, and they can be interpreted in different ways by different people. The phrase that is often used to close a parable was a term in common usage in antiquity, 'let those who have ears to hear, hear.' In short, if you use your head and decipher the subtle hints contained in the parable you will come to the right conclusion. The parables Jesus delivered were very well thought out, generally masterful literary nuggets that to this day have people scratching their heads to unravel the meaning. Probably one of the most interesting and noteworthy realities about the parables, they speak to people today just as well as they applied to the listeners of two millennia ago.

Mark tells us that the 12 disciples had difficulty understanding why Jesus used parables, and he explained that those people who had not been enlightened needed to come to interpretive conclusions on their own, so that one day they may see the truth. A subtext to this entire discussion concerns those that never decipher the meaning of the parables, what happens to them?

Jesus in his ministry made it very clear that people could make a choice and if they chose the Right Way they would find salvation, which meant they would find heaven in their earthly life. Those that consciously chose the Wrong Way would never find the peace that salvation brings, and of course those blind and unquestioning members of society that have been present with us from the beginning of time, those who unthinkingly live their lives by default and are therefore incapable of hearing, will never find the happiness of salvation. When Greek civilization was in its glory Socrates said that the unexamined life was not worth living, a statement that is echoed in the teachings of Jesus.

And so the healing and the teaching continued. Jesus and the disciples headed to Nazareth where Jesus began to teach in the synagogue, the people were initially impressed but immediately started to question who he thought he was, putting on airs. They knew he was a carpenter, the son of Mary and Joseph, with four brothers and likely some sisters, who were living in Nazareth. Recognizing that he would never be accepted on his home turf Jesus went on to the neighbouring villages teaching and healing.

Jesus gave the disciples the authority to cast out foul spirits, and sent them in pairs to proclaim the need for repentance throughout Judea, where they were able to teach and cure the sick. By now the Jewish world was speculating feverishly about the authority that Jesus had and where his power came from. It is not difficult to imagine the frustration and jealousy his success must have engendered in the synagogue leaders.

The concept of reincarnation had always peripherally been part of the Jewish faith, something that was carried forward into the early Christian beliefs until the second century. It was repressed by the iron hand of Irenaeus, a theologian who was determined to create a unified church where orthodoxy reigned. While Jesus lived reincarnation was still considered possible, and the public continue to speculate, as did Herod Antipas, the man who had executed John the Baptist. He Is reported to have believed that Jesus was the reincarnation of the murdered John.

Jesus effectively used this issue about reincarnation as an opportunity to instruct his disciples. He began by asking who the people were saying he was, and the answer came back as John the Baptist, Elijah or

137

one of the other prophets. He then pressed on and asked who they thought he was, and Peter said he was the Messiah. Jesus made no denials but instructed his disciples to tell no one. Jesus, through his disciples, had closed the loop from his entrance as the Son of Man to this emergence as the designated Son of God. He then spoke clearly about what his future would be, and would tolerate no argument from any of the disciples because his path had been established by God.

They entered Jerusalem, Jesus seated on a donkey, while the crowds of followers spread their cloaks and boughs on his path and loudly celebrated his arrival as the one who was heralding the new kingdom. Imagine the despair that the 12 disciples must have been feeling, surrounded by all the levity and joy coming from the celebrants who had no idea what the future would hold. They went directly to the Temple court, something that they had done many times in the past, and as happened every Passover the courtyard was full of money changers and vendors.

These business people were present to facilitate the requirements for sacrificial slaughter that had to be made for each family. The animals used for the sacrifice had to be blessed by the synagogue authorities, and they had blessed all the animals and birds that were available for sale by the vendors, so a devout Jew had no alternatives but to deal at the Temple court. The currency that was necessary to buy the sacrificial offering were coins minted by the Temple, but the normal currency in use on the streets of cosmopolitan Jerusalem were everything but this official Temple currency, so the money changers were doing a brisk and profitable business.

Jesus strode into the Temple courts and starting to disrupt the commercial activity, turning over the tables and generally creating a major scene that would attract everyone's attention. He began preaching against the commercialization of the Temple court, applauded by all the pilgrims there who were being fleeced of their hard earned money to satisfy their religious requirement. The chief priests would certainly see this differently, which is exactly what Jesus wanted. His ministry time was at an end and he would no longer play it safe, he pointedly went out of his way to offend those in power so that he could fulfil his climactic role. Jesus and the disciples then left Jerusalem to avoid immediate arrest, in the interim this provided an opportunity for the word to spread about Jesus's activities in the Temple courts.

The next morning, they walked back into Jerusalem and went directly to the Temple courts. Jesus was immediately confronted by the chief priests and the teachers of the law, which quickly degenerated into a noisy debate. Then Jesus turned back to the watching throng and continued to teach, to the delight of the crowd. Jerusalem was full of pilgrims, many of whom were supporters of Jesus and his message, not a good time for the Temple leaders to act against Jesus, so they bided their time.

In modern times it is difficult to imagine a problem with identifying people, but in the first century the only way sure way was physical recognition by a personal witness. Remember that everyone wore much the same clothing and, unless you were rich enough to afford expensive dyes, the colours were drab. Without distinguishing features like a bushy white beard, a disfiguring scar or missing an eye, a person needed to be specifically identified by someone who knew them. The Temple leaders had their man in Judas Iscariot, but they had to pick their time when they could attract the least attention.

Jesus and his disciples gathered for the Passover meal in a setting that has been captured for posterity in the da Vinci painting of The Last Supper. It was at that dinner that Jesus initiated the breaking of bread and drinking of wine as remembrance of him, the first communion that has been regularly repeated in most Christian congregations and churches since that time. Following dinner they went out up the Mount of Olives, stopping for prayer in the Garden of Gethsemane. As always, they were accompanied by a crowd of people, and undercover Temple guards were part of the group that were milling about Jesus. Judas Iscariot approached Jesus and kissed him, identifying him to the Temple guards who then arrested Jesus. When the disciples offered resistance Jesus called them off because, as far as he was concerned, things were going just as they should. Jesus was taken away to appear before the high priest, the chief priests, the councilors and the teachers of the law.

The Temple authorities were struggling to get enough evidence against Jesus so that they could have him put to death. Mark tells us that the high priest asked him if he was the Christ, the Son of God and Jesus replied affirmatively, which made him a blasphemer of the worst kind and would seal his fate but for one problem. The Temple guards had the power to arrest but they did not have the power to execute anyone, that was the sole right of the Roman procurator Pontius Pilate.

Here is one of those interesting contradictions that we find many places in the New Testament. Herod Antipas had John the Baptist executed to satisfy the whim of his daughter and there were no repercussions, so why could the leaders of the Temple who were collaborators with Herod not do the same to Jesus? Has Mark deliberately misled us to pander to the sensitivities of the governing Romans?

The fact that Jesus had to appear before Pontius Pilate for his trial suggests that Jesus and his many followers were considered to be a potential danger to the stability of the region, and at any time could create a problem for the Roman occupiers. It appears that the Romans deserve much more credit for the arrest of Jesus than the Gospels imply, Jesus and his large following were beginning to make the Romans anxious and Pontius Pilate had a reputation for eliminating problems before they got out of hand. The Temple leaders were probably acting on instructions from their Roman masters, and were only too happy to comply because they welcomed the elimination of Jesus who was challenging and seriously undermining their authority.

4 – Consequences

The Man Who Went to Trial

According to the Gospel accounts, Jesus of Nazareth was going to stand trial before Pontius Pilate based on accusations from the leaders of the religious community, the people that were responsible for maintaining civil order and regulating the social life of the country. But who was this man? Now that we have examined his words and actions over three years of his short life let's review what we know of him.

First and foremost, he was a devout Jew committed to his faith, and he began his ministry claiming that his objective was to speak to the chosen of God, the Hebrews, and bring them the true message that God had for them. He was incredibly well versed in the scriptures which, together with his very quick wit and high intelligence, allowed him to command the attention and respect of those people who would ultimately oppose him.

Jesus was very deliberate in his actions; he was focused on his goal from the time he walked down to the River Jordan to meet John. The story of his public life almost reads like a script, which is exactly what

Jesus intended. His script was taken from the Hebrew Scriptures which we still have as the Old Testament. There were more than a hundred prophecies in those holy books about the coming of the Messiah and the return of glory for the Jewish nation. Jesus needed only to fulfill a few of these prophecies to round out his agenda. When he met John he took the first step, after which he understandably started having misgivings, so he spent some time in the wilderness on introspection and communing with God.

To accomplish his goal Jesus had to be very organized, he was clearly an excellent planner, but successful attainment of his goal also required him to measure his words very carefully and be a shrewd judge of character. At times he was pragmatic and manipulative in his instructions, but all of his actions were goal oriented. There is no doubt that he believed himself to be the chosen one, the Messiah spoken of in the scriptures, and his belief gave him the level of commitment needed to see everything through to the bitter end.

What is incredibly surprising about Jesus was his ability to instill that level of commitment in his followers, many of whom gladly went to their deaths because of their faith. Granted, this was after the resurrection had occurred. Jesus was incredibly charismatic but, without the resurrection, it is doubtful that his followers would have had this level of commitment and the movement would likely have fallen apart. This level of devotion was not just true for the 12 disciples, unknown numbers of committed followers were persecuted, tortured, fed to the lions, massacred and crucified as the ultimate cost of following Jesus' message of redemption.

Admittedly the evidence is thin, but it appears that Jesus was a proponent of equality of sexes at a level that was far above that of the society that created him. He also had incredible tolerance, every place he went he was dogged by followers so that the only time he could get any peace and quiet was when he withdrew to pray. How many of us could do that for three years?

Trial and Punishment - The Son of Man Dies

The next morning the Temple authorities put Jesus in chains and took him to Pilate. The scriptural accounts of the trial with Pontius Pilate are suspect for a number of reasons, including the overwhelming truth that the Romans ruled Judea with an iron fist and would continue to be in that position until well into the third century. Insulting the Romans in any manner would invite retribution, ignoring them would not be much better so it was important for the Gospel writers to cast their role in the best possible light, and we need to be cautious about accepting these accounts at their face value.

Four years after the crucifixion of Jesus Pilate was recalled to Rome because he was unduly cruel in his repression of the rebellion in Samaria, was this the kind of man that would be swayed by the people under his power? I think not, I believe Pilate was more than happy to put an end to the life of the man who enjoyed such a major following that he could one day present a challenge to the Roman government. Rome was not noted for its leniency, it took great pains to foster an atmosphere of fear in the people it had conquered and was always ready to use massacre as a form of crowd control.

Jesus was sentenced to death by crucifixion. While the death sentence would be carried out fairly quickly, the process for the condemned man was torturous in every sense of the word. Whipping, being stripped naked, spat upon, harangued by the ghoulish crowd of sick people who reveled in such things, and forced to carry the cross-member timber to which he would be nailed up the hill to the place of execution. All designed to break the condemned person's spirit and humiliate him. And this is exactly what happened to the condemned man, Jesus of Nazareth.

Mark tells us that there were many women who were followers of Jesus who had come with him to Jerusalem that were present at the execution, and he specifically mentions Mary Magdalene. The corpse was given to Joseph of Arimathea, a follower of Jesus, who had it placed in a tomb cut in the solid rock, and rolled a stone in front of the entrance while Mary Magdalene watched. The execution and burial were all completed on the day before the Sabbath, the day we now call Friday.

The Temple leaders were concerned that followers of Jesus would remove the body and claim that Jesus was risen from the dead, so they had stationed trusted Temple guards to make sure that did not happen. Early in the morning on the day after the Sabbath, the day now called Sunday, Mary Magdalene and two other women went to the tomb with spices and oils so they could anoint the dead body. The Temple guards were still guarding the grounds but the tomb was open and the body was gone.

The Son of God Rises

On that Sunday morning 20 centuries ago the greatest unsolved mystery in human experience began to unfold. The tomb was empty. The crushed and broken corpse that had been the man Jesus had been laid in the tomb following his crucifixion, and despite the presence of Temple guards, the body had gone missing. That by itself was a mystery that would baffle the authorities and, given adequate time, they would have been able to concoct some story to satisfy the masses and put the matter to rest. But there was a complicating factor, the women were greeted by some unknown presence and were given the message that Jesus had risen as he had predicted.

Overwhelmed by what they had seen and heard they immediately left to go to the disciples and tell them what had happened, but suddenly they were confronted by Jesus who told them to tell his followers that he would see them in Galilee. They hurried to find the disciples and tell them everything that had happened, but the disciples dismissed it as nonsense. We should not judge these men too harshly, they had taken three years out of their lives and left their families and past lives behind to follow Jesus, and now the man they thought was the deliverer of Israel was dead. Imagine the despair that must have filled their hearts, and now they were being confronted by these hysterical women with overactive imaginations! We must remember that women had a very secondary role in Jewish society, and the disciples would have had a very difficult time accepting the fact that Jesus appeared to the women first, so obviously it was nonsense. Later that morning they did go to the tomb and saw that it was empty, but they did not encounter Jesus.

Luke tells us that two of the disciples were journeying to a nearby town later that day, and were joined by a stranger who revealed himself to be Jesus. They immediately returned to Jerusalem to give the good news to the other nine disciples. Did this really happen or was it just part of the storytelling that Luke was engaged in? It really does not matter because all the disciples returned to Galilee as they had been instructed by the Son of Man before his death. While they were gathered there Jesus appeared to them and the disciples became convinced that the Son of God had risen.

Collaborating Evidence

This was a mystery that could not be solved. The body was missing and never was found, despite the best efforts of the Temple leaders who had a vested interest in discrediting this story. This was not simply a matter of tracking down a lost corpse, the real issue was the reappearance of Jesus as a spirit who could interact with people and had beaten death. What other evidence do we have to offer to support this resurrection story?

The most obvious first question is whether or not Jesus really died on the cross? The Romans generally let the bodies remain hanging until they rotted as a warning to others, but in this case Joseph of Arimathea was able to collect the body within a few hours of the death and place it in a tomb. Why was he allowed to do this? He was a wealthy and well respected member of the Jewish community who made a personal plea to Pilate which was granted, subject to the death being verified. Pilate sent a soldier to see it Jesus was dead, when it was confirmed the body was released. The Romans were experts at killing people and would never make such an error, Jesus did indeed die.

We also need to look at the number of instances when Jesus the spirit appeared.

– The women as they left the tomb
– The evening of the resurrection, two disciples on the road
– A few days later, the disciples in Galilee
– Three or four years later, Saul of Tarsus on the road to Damascus
– In his letter to the Galatians Paul talks about the risen Jesus appearing to 500 people

Then there is the external evidence, the reality that neither the Temple leaders nor the Roman occupiers were able to debunk the story of the resurrection speaks volumes. They both had an incredibly compelling vested interest in disproving the claim and, despite having all the resources imaginable available to them, were unsuccessful. This is clearly supported by the work of contemporary historians. Josephus, the Jewish historian who lived through the time of Jesus' execution. Later the Roman historian Tacitus confirmed the facts of Jesus' life and times, and the claims about the resurrection. Here is an interesting letter that shows the incredible commitment of the early Christians, Faith that can only result from a profound belief in the veracity of the resurrection.

In about 112 A.D. the Roman governor of what is now northern Turkey wrote to Emperor Trajan regarding the Christians in his district:

"I was never present at any trial of Christians; therefore I do not know what are the customary penalties or investigations, and what limits are observed. . . whether those who recant should be pardoned. . . whether the name itself, even if innocent of crime, should be punished, or only the crimes attaching to that name. . . . Meanwhile, this is the course that I have adopted in the case of those brought before me as Christians. I ask them if they are Christians. If they admit it I repeat the question a second and a third time, threatening capital punishment; if they persist I sentence them to death. For I do not doubt that, whatever kind of crime it may be to which they have confessed, their pertinacity and inflexible obstinacy should certainly be punished. . . the very fact of my dealing with the question led to a wider spread of the charge, and a great variety of cases were brought before me. An

anonymous pamphlet was issued, containing many names. All who denied that they were or had been Christians I considered should be discharged, because they called upon the gods at my dictation and did reverence. . .and especially because they cursed Christ, a thing which it is said, genuine Christians cannot be induced to do."

What Happened?

2000 years later we cannot begin to explain what happened. Is it simply because our science has not progressed far enough and, given time, we will be able to explain and understand this phenomena? If that is the case, then how on earth could someone utilize this as yet unidentified science 2000 years ago? They simply could not have done so, what happened was so extraordinary and beyond our human comprehension in the first and the 21st century that we need to look outside ourselves and our modern secular mindset.

The first century world had four dimensions, the three that we can see and a fourth of the spirit that was used by the devout to communicate with their maker. In the 21st century we know there are many more dimensions to our lives than we can see and touch, and our scientists are constantly discovering new ones. Solar radiation is a perfect example, it penetrates everything and passes through our bodies, and yet without science we would never have known anything about it. And intuition, how many of us have gone into a room and immediately sensed something different in the air? What about ghosts? Not the spooky kind that we find in horror stories, but the kind that people are increasingly ready to admit they have experienced. On a number of occasions, I have been aware of the presence of bodiless others, and the result has always been positive and comforting, what about you? For most people who are truly honest with themselves it is not difficult to accept the concept of ghosts, so why must we labour over the question of what happened? We just need to accept that something extraordinary and unexplainable happened that defies our humancentric understanding.

The real questions are about what happened with the body, who rolled away the stone and why did the Temple guards not see any of this happening? If it was divine intervention, then why the physical evidence about the stone door and the disappearance of the body? Because human beings need convincing proof and physical proof is as good as it gets. That really explains why the Christian story took the world by storm when so many other well meaning prophets and their messages have been lost in the dust of time, irrefutable proof.

5 – Growing Pains

From the Jordan River to Jerusalem

What happened between the day Jesus left his family in Nazareth and he met John the Baptist at the Jordan River? Some scholars suggest he was with the Essenes, the mystical Jewish sect, because of philosophical similarities in such things as the commonality of property, disdain for wealth and finery, and his emphasis on repentance. It should come as no surprise that this sounds a little like the preaching of John the Baptist, who almost certainly was a member of this apocalyptic sect. The number of Essenes was never very large so we can be sure that Jesus and John knew each other before their historic meeting, remember that John immediately recognized Jesus according to the Gospel accounts.

Later in the Gospel stories we are told that Jesus, on hearing that John the Baptist had been arrested, started to proclaim that the kingdom of heaven was at hand and people should repent. Based on our analysis of the words of Jesus we did not find any examples of Jesus making this claim, but it is an easy extrapolation that we can confidently say would have been made by the members of the early Jesus Movement, and recorded for posterity by Matthew.

John the Baptist had been preaching repentance and baptizing people for some time before Jesus arrived on the scene, and had developed quite a following in the Judaic community. With the sharp exchange of words that went on between Jesus and the Pharisees following his baptism, words that were heard by all those present, it is very likely that followers trailed in his path as he walked up the hill from the river. They would have dropped off when he returned to the wilderness for his time of contemplation, but we can be sure that they told everyone about the event. By the time Jesus re-entered society news of his baptism and John's reaction, together with his daring response to the presence of the Pharisees keeping an eye on John, meant that he would have been immediately recognizable wherever he turned up. Crowds would gather where he started to teach and inevitably some of those hangers on would follow him as he moved through the countryside. Just as a snowball becomes an avalanche, the group of followers continued to swell.

Early in his ministry Jesus recruited disciples so his entourage of committed people was large enough to attract attention wherever it went. It did not take very long before the size of his following meant that Jesus was also being watched by the Pharisees, and the crowds were large enough to permit Temple spies to move around with anonymity. We can imagine that the scene would be very little different from a public happening today. The core group of supporters would be there, other people with an interest in what was happening in their community would come out for the event and passersby would stop for a while, listen and then move on.

Jesus and his roving band would have been of sufficient size to attract attention, but it certainly would not have been great hordes of people because the towns and villages he was visiting would not have the capacity to feed and house too many. Whenever he has been accompanied by large crowds we can safely assume that these crowds were day travelers who, hearing about the coming event, made a special trip from their village or town. Another thing we must consider is the weather, Jesus' ministry lasted three years and Israel has a temperate climate, which means that it gets four distinctively different seasons. In the winter it is wet and cold, sometimes cold enough to snow, so it is very likely that the pace of his ministry would vary with the seasons. Unfortunately, the Gospel and historical accounts are silent on this subject, so we will have to presume what should be obvious. In the worst of the winter Jesus and the disciples would have taken a break to find refuge, perhaps they even returned to their homes. This would have provided a needed hiatus for Jesus and his disciples from the constant pressures of the crowd and the ever present scrutiny of the Temple guards.

As Jesus and the disciples continued their travels on what was likely a circuit not unlike those used today by traveling entertainers, their reputation as teachers and skewers of the Pharisees would grow, so the crowds turning out to see him would increase dramatically over time. His growing popularity and ability to sidestep every attempt to discredit him must have made life intolerable for the Pharisees and Temple leaders.

The Crucial Turning Point

Jesus was not the first Hebrew prophet to develop a large following and he certainly was not the last. His martyrdom was something that he shared with a number of other prophets and leaders, an event that usually resulted in the death of their movement. For the followers of Jesus, the people of The Way, many of whom had given up so much of their lives before they met Jesus, his death must have been a crushingly brutal fact to accept. Imagine the despondency of several thousand people for whom their world had just fallen apart, the disbelief, the emptiness, the heartache.

They would have flocked to the synagogue on the Sabbath following the execution looking for some hope, but seeing all the eyes that surround them filled with the same blankness and despair must have been devastating. And then another sleepless night before the dawning of the day that they knew would be one of decision for them, how could they recover their lost lives and go back to a normal lifestyle?

He is risen! Can you imagine how quickly the word would have spread around

Jerusalem that the grave was empty and the body was gone? Followers would be rushing to find their comrades and give them the amazing news, others would be speculating about how the disciples were able to steal the body away under the noses of the Temple guards. The entire city would soon be abuzz with the news, the Temple leaders would be huddled in frantic discussions about how to contain the furour and come up with an explanation to defuse the situation. But they could not, the Temple guards who had been selected because of their fierce loyalty to the Temple were adamant in their defense. They could find no scapegoat, no one to blame for perpetuating a hoax about the resurrection story.

As the silence from the synagogue stretched past the first day the speculation grew, and by the end of the week even those people loyal to the Temple were having second thoughts. The masses who had followed Jesus were jubilant and full of hope. Their numbers were swelling each day as undecided people who had been waiting to see what would happen considered the evidence and decided in favour of the Jesus Movement. While the Roman overseers would have been keeping a close eye on the events they would not intervene unless a political threat arose, and were undoubtedly amused by the consternation of the Temple hierarchy.

The resurrection was the flame that lit the kindling, and what would follow fanned the flames even higher.

Unleashing the Devil

It is almost impossible for us to imagine the impact that the living Jesus and his message had on the poor and downtrodden Hebrew people of Jerusalem. The culture of poverty and disenfranchisement in a conquered society had existed for five hundred years, more than 20 generations of people who had no hope. There was virtually no opportunity for people at the lowest level of society to better themselves short of turning to crime, which was an even faster way to an early death.

And then came Jesus with his message of hope. Hope, something these people never dared to think about. Jesus gave them hope, they caught the spirit of his message and were looking forward to a new world unfolding in the very near future; his execution caused unbelievable, gut wrenching angst as the people who would benefit most from his triumphs came to grips with the reality that it was all over. Their hopes had turned to dust.

They barely had an opportunity to get used to the idea that the hope for a better future was over, then the news came. The tomb was empty! The news spread like wildfire across the city and igniting hope once again in the hearts of all those who had despaired over Jesus' death. Over the next couple of days the word filtered downward from the apostles that they had seen Jesus! He had risen as he said he would, coming to fulfill his promises to the world. Hallelujah! All those despondent hearts were reignited by the flame of faith, hope was restored.

Many of these followers came from the lower ranks of the Jerusalem social structure and likely did not attend the synagogue, they were not welcome. They were poor, primarily semiliterate and certainly not very well educated about the Hebrew Scriptures. They definitely did not fit in with the relatively affluent crowd that attended services each Sabbath.

The Temple establishment made a strategic mistake that benefited the Jesus Movement enormously. After the resurrection the synagogue continued to operate as before, content to let the disenfranchised rabble remain on the fringes of the Jewish faith. Rather than welcome them as Jews that had returned to the fold and using this as an opportunity, the established power base did their best to continue to exclude and marginalize them. These people, the hopeless who had been given hope, were quick to embrace the Jesus Movement because it was the only option they had for breaking out of the cage of drudgery and hopelessness that was their life.

On the other hand, those Jews who were part of the synagogue structure and embraced the teachings of Jesus, followers of The Way, continued to participate in the synagogue activities as a tolerated sect of the Hebrew faith. This was not an unprecedented situation, the Hebrew faith had a tradition of successive prophets from its very beginning, and it was not uncommon for followers to incorporate their teachings within their established faith.

Those who had seen some hope for their desperate situation and were reignited by news of the resurrection were not prepared to fold their tents and go back to their life of deprivation. Leaders emerged who seized on the words of Jesus and inflamed the crowds, emphasizing his teachings that the disciples should go out and accept hospitality wherever it is offered. Within a short time, there were roving bands of zealous followers of The Way moving across Israel, preaching and living off the land as they went. In no time these groups became a pariah amongst the landed Jewish followers of the Jesus Movement, who would find themselves the unwilling hosts of a dozen people camped in their courtyard.

This created an opportunity that was too good to resist for a number of opportunistic people who saw it as a way to escape poverty, soon there developed roving bands that were primarily focused on theft and exploitation under the guise of finding religious fulfillment.

It is no surprise that all these people would be lumped into a single category, Jesus Movement Jews, without distinguishing between those of real faith and those who were using it as a cover for their activities. These ne'er-do-well groups gave the orthodox Hebrew establishment the ammunition it needed to begin persecution of this disruptive Jesus sect. They were determined to contain it before it became a force that required Roman intervention.

This policy had an unplanned but totally acceptable result as far as the Temple leaders were concerned, it drove many of the Jesus sect Jews out of Jerusalem into other centres of the civilized world. This migration was really quite easy for the followers of The Way, over preceding generations Jewish traders and merchants had established communities along the trade routes and in the cities of antiquity, so these emigrating Jews would easily find a welcome from the Jewish diaspora that existed in the first century CE.

The Jewish Response

Without much encouragement the keepers of the law jumped on the bandwagon to stamp out this heresy that was depleting their congregation and causing so much embarrassment to the Temple leaders. Using the roving gangs of pseudo Jesus Movement people as an excuse, they began to actively persecute followers of The Way. They passed Temple laws banning the sect and then delegated Temple agents to root out and prosecute the errant Jews who were part of the Jesus Movement.

One of these agents was Saul of Tarsus, son of an established and respected family in the synagogue, who also happened to be a Roman citizen because of his father's connections. By this time the punishment for Jewish followers of this heresy was very significant. These roving mobs were also a concern to the Roman occupiers, and it was not very long before Rome decided that followers of The Way constituted a threat to Rome, and the persecution, which now had official government sanction, intensified and carried the penalty of death.

Jockeying for Control

The base of the Jesus Movement was in Jerusalem led by Peter, the first disciple, and James the brother of Jesus. Peter and James were both devout Jews and they saw the movement begun by Jesus as a logical extension of the Hebrew faith. Jesus had specifically stated that he was there to bring the Jewish people back into a meaningful relationship with God, making no mention of Gentile followers. Peter and James followed that dictum to the letter. Followers of The Way had to follow the religious laws set out in the Hebrew Scriptures with respect to dietary and hygienic practices which, for all intent and purposes, meant that they had to be devout Jews first and then a follower of the Jesus Movement second.

Three or four years after the crucifixion the Temple heresy hunter, Saul of Tarsus, was on his way to Damascus to track down some errant followers of The Way. His journey was interrupted by a life changing experience. Blazing lights, temporary blindness and visions of Jesus speaking to him resulted in Saul the persecutor becoming Paul, the follower of The Way.

Eventually Paul's thinking became a fundamental element in the development of Christianity as a religion separate and distinct from Judaism. In the formative years following his conversion he came to a conclusion that was totally contrary to that held by Peter and James. Paul believed that Jesus and his message liberated people from the burdens of the Hebrew laws as they entered into a new relationship with a God of love. Paul then went further, insisting that he had been recruited by the risen Jesus to carry the good news to the Jews and Gentiles, if Paul's converts had to

169

abide by the criteria set out by Peter and James that meant that the Gentiles had to effectively become Jewish in all respects.

This created a major philosophical problem in the developing movement, two viewpoints that were diametrical opposites. This was not simply a difference of opinion, both groups were off doing their own thing without any coordination between the two factions. Peter and James in Jerusalem, focused on developing the Jesus Movement in the Jewish community as an offshoot of the traditional Hebrew faith. Paul in the hinterland, making converts in the distant Jewish communities who were culturally Jewish but had lived for years beyond the spiritual reach of Jerusalem.

This got even more complicated when Paul started converting Gentiles, why on earth would they ever want to adopt the very restrictive Jewish lifestyle as a condition for becoming a follower of The Way? Although Jesus had originally stipulated that his message was for the Jews, there are accounts in the Gospels of him interacting with Gentile believers, and he made no stipulation that they become Jews to become his followers. On the other hand, Jesus had stated that he had come to uphold the law, not displace it. Paul was following the precedent set by the actions of Jesus whereas Peter and James were adhering to his spoken words. The fact that Jesus appears to have said one thing and then acted in another way underscores the Son of Man's humanity.

In an effort to resolve the conflict Paul went to Jerusalem to meet with James and Peter, but remained only two weeks before he returned to his work in the field. The two polarities were not reconciled for several years, so for a time there were these two streams of the Christian faith developing independently, separated by geography and ideology. These two factions continued to develop in splendid isolation until the persecution of followers of The Way escalated 14 years after the crucifixion, resulting in the execution of James while Peter escaped.

Six years later the persecution had ended and a conference was held in Jerusalem to resolve this critical issue that threatened to split the developing faith. It was agreed that Gentiles were to be welcomed into the movement, exempt from the Hebrew dietary requirements and circumcision. Peter undoubtedly would have attended this conference and it is likely that he was still based in Jerusalem, taking up residence in Rome at a later date. He did travel extensively after he was forced to flee Jerusalem in 44 CE, his travels are not well documented but he did spend some time with Paul. Peter eventually arrived in Rome where he was imprisoned and crucified 34 years after the death of Jesus. When Peter was executed Paul was in a Roman prison, so the leadership of the Jesus Movement was taken over by the second generation of Christians who are commonly referred to as the Apostolic Fathers.

40 Years Later

This is probably the earliest known broadly based, grassroots movement in the history of mankind, and without a doubt the most successful. Rooted as it was in the Hebrew culture, the relentless persecution by the Jewish leaders created an environment where this Judaic sect increasingly distanced itself from its roots. Paul was instrumental in creating a church structure that was a direct duplication of the tried and true synagogue system, one that had stood the test of time and ensured that the Jewish people survived and prospered culturally and spiritually despite the travails of history.

One does not have to look very far to validate that claim. Whatever happened to the Assyrians, Babylonians, Phoenicians, the lost tribes of Israel? Obviously they got assimilated into other cultures, but the point is they lost their language, cultural and religious identity while the Jewish nation protected their language, religion and culture for at least 2000 years before Jesus arrived on the scene, and continue to do so to this day.

40 years later would be the year 70 CE, which was the year that the Roman authorities put down another Jewish revolt and destroyed the Temple in Jerusalem. That had a very important impact on the development of the Christian church, the umbilical cord back to its Jewish roots was severed. The importance of the work done by Paul grew, which seriously reduced the reliance on the Old Testament doctrines for the followers of The Way.

Tolerance of the new faith by the Roman Empire depended very much on the power struggles back in Rome. Each Emperor was absolute and their likes and dislikes were immediately echoed throughout the empire, resulting in major change resonating on a regular basis through the civilized world under Roman control. Everything from fashion styles to games played, how you treated your slaves and the treatment accorded to indigenous religions of the conquered peoples depended on the whims of the Emperor of the moment.

The armed Jewish revolt that had culminated in the destruction of the Temple set off a wave of intolerance and persecution of Jews throughout the empire. The new Christian sect was particularly troublesome to the Romans, it was expanding quickly and welcoming Gentiles into the fold in every major centre in the empire, even in Rome. Wherever the new faith spread waves of persecution and tolerance followed, like ripples on a pond.

About this time the Gospel of Mark was written by a Jew residing in Rome, providing the first real written history about what happened, based on the missing document 'Q' and the oral tradition that continued to be an important factor in communicating for several centuries. There is another document that warrants our attention, one that came out of the oral tradition and apparently was first put in written form in the middle of the first century. The first version of the Didache formed the basis for church doctrine until the middle of the second century, endlessly added to and expanded, but it does give us a very clear picture of how the followers of The Way conducted themselves.

6 – Followers of The Way

What Did the Followers Believe?

In the absence of specific written documentation, we need to look at the actions taken by these followers in the 40 years after Jesus' crucifixion. Paul, the driving force behind the development of the Christian church, was executed in 68 CE, so his teachings as documented in his many letters are critical to this understanding. Since all of his letters predate the accepted Gospels of the New Testament they are probably the most reliable source that we can use to achieve our objective.

On the other hand, we must not place too much reliance on the theological interpretations because his ideas were not widely circulated for a number of years, and only started to have a significant impact on Christian teachings early in the second century. Paul did make a very important contribution to the new movement at the very earliest stages however, it was he who structured the system of churches with a Bishop overseeing several congregations, an innovation that was quickly adopted everywhere.

There is no disputing their unconditional acceptance of the resurrection, for these early Christians that was a simple fact. With so many eyewitness accounts and no evidence to the contrary ever being provided by those who would like to discredit it, the resurrection was simply a reality. They celebrated communion, believed adult baptism by immersion was a physical expression of being reborn to a new life and was a critical step that everyone had to follow. Community was an integral part of their support structure and, thanks to Paul and his great organizational ability, the community of believers had an internal support system that served its members very well.

In our modern Western society where families and friends are divided by thousands of miles we have lost much of our sense of community. We apparently have also lost our basic need for community as a survival tool and replaced it with technology, structured medical care and a plethora of ways to keep us occupied. Or have we really lost our basic need for community? I think not, we have simply replaced the intensely personal community of the past with a controlled, often impersonal system of clubs, churches and activities that fulfill our need for feeling we are part of a community. It is very difficult for us to understand how important community was to the people in antiquity, the majority of whom lived their lives and died in the local area where they were born. This would be of much greater importance to those who were marginalized through the accident of birth. The appeal of a faith community must have been incredibly strong to the disenfranchised especially, and this certainly contributed significantly to the development of congregations of people united by faith rather than birthright.

What did they think of heaven? Were they content to accept heaven on earth as Jesus had taught or were they looking at the prospect of a better afterlife of the idyllic kind created by the established church in the second and third centuries? No one really knows, but the message of salvation and pending judgment must have been at the core of their teachings. Whether they were motivated to join The Way because of their hopes for a future life after death or because they wanted to have a better quality of life that had meaning to God is inconsequential, it almost certainly did have a profound impact on the quality of their life on earth by providing them with peace of mind.

Of course they definitely believed in the Two Ways, the Way of Life and the Way of Death. By selecting the Way of Life they followed the prohibitions and responsibilities of the oral tradition that was later set down in the Didache. As we review these rules for living there are two important things to note. In the very last notation the reference is made to sons and daughters rather than just sons, which was inconsistent with the prevailing Judaic culture. Secondly, the text is totally gender neutral so it will apply to men and women equally. This suggests that the culture of the people of The Way regarded men and women as equals, and where did they get that understanding if not from Jesus and his disciples? In the early church women frequently took leadership roles.

There are also two important omissions that are noteworthy. There is no mention anywhere against homosexual relationships, although we know that this was not tolerated by the Judaic faith. The apostle Paul was vehemently homophobic, in many of his letters he has added homosexuality to the list of proscribed activities. Why would he be inclined to do that unless homosexuality was accepted by the followers of The Way and he disagreed with it? That raises the larger question of why Paul had such a problem with it, but that is a question for Pauline scholars to answer.

The second significant omission concerns divorce, although it is mentioned in the Gospels in the harshest of terms it does not appear to have been a concern of Jesus or his followers. On the surface that is not surprising, becoming a follower of The Way was a personal decision and we can easily imagine that it resulted in destroying some marriages and family relationships. That is good news for people of faith in our modern society where divorce rates are so high, becoming divorced is not a sin.

The first version of the Didache – Teaching of the Apostles – was available in the early church about the middle of the first century and was continually updated into the early second century. The document had been built in layers and it is only the first six chapters that appear to represent a summary of the teachings of the earliest organization, while it was still a sect of the Hebrew faith.

Unfortunately, we cannot say categorically that these six chapters are as they were first written, they too may have been overlaid with amendments and adjustments by the early church fathers as they tightened their control over the ranks of believers. Within the first six chapters of the second century version we have today there are passages and sections that clearly relate to situations, circumstances and challenges in the emerging church that arose early in its development. The complete Didache is included in the appendices.

The teachings of the Two Ways are very clearly set out here, and apparently were taken from the lost document that is referred to in many first and second century texts. From the very beginning this document was not meant to be a statement of faith, it is a prescription for living that very clearly reflects the teachings of Jesus. It establishes an acceptable lifestyle that reflects and reinforces Judaic values, but determinatively differentiates followers of The Way from the influences of the Roman and Hellenistic cultures that were so pervasive in Asia Minor.

And that raises a very interesting question, for the early Jewish sect that would later be called Christians where is a statement of faith? From antiquity until today every faith stream has criteria for membership that are rigorously enforced, so is it not reasonable to expect that the early Christians would have a similar pattern? But that does not appear to be the case, the early Christians clearly modelled their criteria for membership based on acceptance of the teachings of Jesus, which emphasized looking at how a person lived rather than what they professed. That is why the Didache sets out no faith criteria, each person had to walk the walk and talk the talk; by focusing on rules to live by this document imposes lifestyle expectations that would only be attractive to people of faith who are prepared to make the sacrifices needed to follow The Way.

The first six chapters of the Didache follow, they best represent what was really important to the first Christians, the entire document from the second century is included in the appendix.

Chapter 1. The Two Ways and the first Commandment

There are two ways, one of life and one of death, but a great difference between the two ways. The way of life, then, is this: first, you shall love God who made you; second, love your neighbour as yourself, and do not do to another what you would not want done to you. And of these sayings the teaching is this: Bless those who curse you, and pray for your enemies, and fast for those who persecute you. For what reward is there for loving those who love you? Do not the Gentiles do the same? But love those who hate you, and you shall not have an enemy. Abstain from fleshly and worldly lusts. If someone strikes your right cheek, turn to him the other also, and you shall be perfect. If someone impresses you for one mile, go with him two. If someone takes your cloak, give him also your coat. If someone takes from you what is yours, ask it not back, for indeed you are not able. Give to everyone who asks you, and ask it not back; for the Father wills that to all should be given of our own blessings (free gifts). Happy is he who gives according to the commandment, for he is guiltless. Woe to him who receives; for if one receives who has need, he is guiltless; but he who receives not having need shall pay the penalty, why he received and for what. And coming into confinement, he shall be examined concerning the things which he has done, and he shall not escape from there until he pays back the last penny. And also concerning this, it has been said, Let your alms sweat in your hands, until you know to whom you should give.

In this single, lengthy paragraph they pick up quite a collection of the original sayings of Jesus that we have identified in part one of this book. This appears to have been first written about 50 CE, and would likely have relied heavily on the oral tradition that was the only means available to transfer information quickly in the early first century. We can trust this tradition for two reasons, it is based on the disciplined approach that is endemic to the Hebrew culture and religion and it is collaborated by much of the documentation we have seen in part one of this book. It all fits together very nicely.

Chapter 2. The Second Commandment: Grave Sin Forbidden

And the second commandment of the Teaching; You shall not commit murder, you shall not commit adultery, you shall not commit pederasty, you shall not commit fornication, you shall not steal, you shall not practice magic, you shall not practice witchcraft, you shall not murder a child by abortion nor kill that which is born. You shall not covet the things of your neighbour, you shall not swear, you shall not bear false witness, you shall not speak evil, you shall bear no grudge. You shall not be double-minded nor double-tongued, for to be double-tongued is a snare of death. Your speech shall not be false, nor empty, but fulfilled by deed. You shall not be covetous, nor rapacious, nor a hypocrite, nor evil disposed, nor haughty. You shall not take evil counsel against your neighbour. You shall not hate any man; but some you shall reprove, and concerning some you shall pray, and some you shall love more than your own life.

This section deals with things you should not do, and there is no doubt that it reflects the realities that existed in the first century where numerous cultures existed in close proximity and, because of the Roman tolerance for established religions that accepted the rule of Rome, a broad range of religious beliefs and practices of these different cultures coexisted. Chapter 2 is in many ways a reflection of the Judaic heritage that was the starting point for the followers of The Way, and a repudiation of the practices of other religions of antiquity.

Pederasty is a word that is almost never used in a modern context and warrants explanation. In Greek and Roman society, it was not unusual nor unacceptable for men to have long term relationships with boys, and the mentoring and education the boy received would often give him an advantage as he grew to be an adult, when he would repeat the cycle by taking his own boy consort. In those societies this was not considered pedophilia because children were virtually without rights, and parents wishing to advance their sons' prospects were often willing participants. This was not acceptable in the Jewish culture and notably was never adopted by the group known as Hellenistic Jews, the Sadducees, although they were heavily influenced by other aspects of the Greek culture.

It is important to note the exceptions such as divorce, although perhaps it was not a major problem in a society where the life expectancy was so very short. The fact that it is not prohibited implies that it was accepted. The same can be said about homosexuality and prostitution, human realities that existed in that society and continue to be part of our social fabric in the 21st century.

Chapter 3. Other Sins Forbidden

Flee from every evil thing, and from every likeness of it. Be not prone to anger, for anger leads to murder. Be neither jealous, nor quarrelsome, nor of hot temper, for out of all these murders are engendered. Be not a lustful one for lust leads to fornication. Be neither a filthy talker, nor of lofty eye, for out of all these adulteries are engendered. Be not an observer of omens, since it leads to idolatry. Be neither an enchanter, nor an astrologer, nor a purifier, nor be willing to look at these things, for out of all these idolatry is engendered. Be not a liar, since a lie leads to theft. Be neither money-loving, nor vainglorious, for out of all these thefts are engendered.

Chapter 4. Various Precepts

Do not long for division, but rather bring those who contend to peace. Judge righteously, and do not respect persons in reproving for transgressions. You shall not be undecided whether or not it shall be. Be not a stretcher forth of the hands to receive and a drawer of them back to give. If you have anything, through your hands you shall give ransom for your sins. Do not hesitate to give, nor complain when you give; for you shall know who is the good repayer of the hire. Do not turn away from him who is in want; rather, share all things with your brother, and do not say that they are your own. For if you are partakers in that which is immortal, how much more in things which are mortal? Do not remove your hand from your son or daughter; rather, teach them the fear of God from their youth.

Chapter 5. The Way of Death

And the way of death is this: first of all it is evil and accursed: murders, adultery, lust, fornication, thefts, idolatries, magic arts, witchcrafts, rape, false witness, hypocrisy, double-heartedness, deceit, haughtiness, depravity, self-will, greediness, filthy talking, jealousy, over-confidence, loftiness, boastfulness; persecutors of the good, hating truth, loving a lie, not knowing a reward for righteousness, not cleaving to good nor to help righteous judgment, watching not for that which is good, but for that which is evil; from whom meekness and endurance are far, loving vanities, pursuing revenge, not pitying a poor man, not labouring for the afflicted, not knowing Him Who made them, murderers of children, destroyers of the handiwork of God, turning away from him who is in want, afflicting him who is distressed, advocates of the rich, lawless judges of the poor, utter sinners. Be delivered, children, from all these.

Chapter 6. Against False Teachers, and Food Offered to Idols

See that no one causes you to err from this way of the Teaching, since apart from God it teaches you. For if you are able to bear the entire yoke of the Lord, you will be perfect; but if you are not able to do this, do what you are able. And concerning food, bear what you are able; but against that which is sacrificed to idols be exceedingly careful; for it is the service of dead gods.

Towards an Uncertain Future

The destruction of the Temple in Jerusalem in 70 CE had a major impact on the Judaic faith, but it also signaled the final schism between the Christian sect and the Jewish faith. At this time there were still many people with a foot in both camps who were now forced to make a painful decision, do they return to the faith of their fathers or do they join the followers of The Way? For the Hellenistic Jews, the Sadducees, the question was very simple to answer. They had an intense orientation toward the holy Temple, and its destruction created a vacuum at the centre of their faith. Followers of The Way, on the other hand, were establishing churches along the same model that synagogues had used for millennia and the Sadducees quickly embraced the new emerging faith stream.

But where to from here? The Romans remained in control of the known world for another three centuries and Roman persecution of both Jews and Christians varied widely, depending on the whims of the sitting Roman Emperor. Over several hundred years Jewish merchants and traders had created a Jewish diaspora in virtually every major centre in the Levant, North Africa and Southern Europe. Jesus made it clear that his first priority was to bring his message to the members of the Hebrew faith, and as a new Jewish sect the message of The Way would have been carried to all these congregations. The first apostles targeted Jewish populations and only later, after the definitive conference in Jerusalem in 50 CE, were Gentiles openly welcomed into the new faith.

Christianity had been beset by differences of opinion and splintering from its very beginning, best illustrated by the fundamental differences between the church in Jerusalem led by Peter and James and the churches being established in other communities by Paul. After Peter's imprisonment and execution in Rome the seat of the church remained in Rome, although Christian theologians sprang up across the churches with the role of the Bishop of Rome one of coordination rather than the dispensation of power. Eventually these various approaches to being a Christian would be subjected to critical review and heresies would be purged by the sword, thanks in large part to the second century Bishop of Lyon and theologian Irenaeus.

7 – Answers & More Questions

The Really Big Questions

When I began this exploratory journey I had three primary questions that I wanted to answer. As I was studying the documents that are available and reflecting on the meaning that this has for me, I came up with a number of other questions that led me even further down the investigative path. As these questions were resolved in my own mind I tried to reflect the results in the narrative that I have provided in this book. Hopefully I did not answer all the questions you might have, my purpose is to encourage you to undertake your own faith study, determine who you really are and what makes you a unique human being.

I could not fully answer all my questions, does that mean I failed in my quest? I think not, in some cases I was asking questions for which there is no answer and determining that reality is functionally an answer of sorts. Nevertheless, I am happy to share my findings with you. And now my questions.

1 Jesus, his apostles and other followers were, through their faith, able to perform many miracles including healing the sick,

casting out demons and bringing people back to life. This ability seems to have disappeared as that first generation died, not even Paul who was personally selected by Jesus to carry his message to the Gentiles had this power. What happened?

This fundamental question is one that I have not been able to answer, and that is very perplexing because without an answer to that question everything else is placed in doubt. I accept the fact that Jesus and his followers were, through their faith, able to perform all kinds of extraordinary miracles as so thoroughly documented historically. What happened to that power, was it specifically intended to have limited life until the spark that Jesus struck turned into a roaring fire? As the Son of Man Jesus did state that he was setting the fire and was going to be around long enough to make sure it was burning well.

That would explain why Paul was never given that power, and the fact that he did not complain about that inability suggests that Jesus, in his conversation with Paul on the road to Damascus, made it very clear how it was to be. It also explains another unasked but obvious question; why did Jesus not continue appearing to the faithful after the first few years following his execution? Is that because his job was done or is it because the message that he so eloquently delivered had become so contorted over time that he was washing his hands of the whole mess?

2 Who was this man Jesus and what was his real message, unembellished by the editors and revisionists of antiquity?

Jesus was clearly a man of the people, born, raised and living amongst his peers. He was surrounded by pain and deprivation, hallmarks of the time in which he was living, aggravated by the almost unbearable burden of exploitation by the Roman occupiers. He was well educated in the Temple tradition, exceedingly bright and very reflective, without a doubt a very spiritual man who was fully committed to serving God. He had human parents, brothers and probably sisters. As a devout Jew he would have followed the regular rites of passage and been married by his early 20s. There is no record of him having children, if he did they would surely have been present at his crucifixion with their grandmother. Perhaps his wife died in childbirth or the marriage was childless.

194

The humanity of Jesus is readily apparent in his words and actions. He was generally very careful and specific in choosing his words so that they could not be twisted around and used against him. Early in his ministry, when he was feeling full of compassion for his followers who were among the most oppressed in their society, he said many things to comfort them and thereby build his following. The Beatitudes are a compilation of these words of comfort that were likely delivered by Jesus as one liners throughout his early ministry.

Jesus was as manipulative as any person could be, engineering his progress to Golgotha in accordance with the scriptural prophecies so that he could fulfill his destiny of becoming the spiritual Messiah. On the other hand, his unwavering commitment to his goal over a three year period, and his tolerance for being continually surrounded by throngs of people, were superhuman.

His message was incredibly simple and straightforward for those that would listen. Jesus often used the expression "let those who have ears to hear, hear", stressing that his parables had hidden messages for those who were spiritually receptive. At the risk of being accused of overt simplification his core message was:

- Love and trust in God.
- Treat other people the way you want to be treated.
- Heaven and hell are part of our lives, we make the choice of how we want to live.

3 Why did this particular Jewish sect succeed in transforming the ancient world and survive through the ages to have a major formative influence on the development of Western civilization?

The answer to the first part of this question comes directly from any modern marketing textbook, the two most important factors in making the introduction of any new product successful are timing and how the market perceives the product. They have to happen in synchronistic harmony or the new product will not be successfully received, and that is exactly what happened with the Jesus Movement. The timing was perfect and the message of hope was exactly what the people wanted to hear.

The answer to the second part of the question is complicated, but easy to understand when one considers how the dynamics of greed and power shaped the history of the Western world. The history of humankind from the very beginning is all about greed and power, our incapacity to learn from past mistakes is almost beyond comprehension.

The timing was right everywhere in the known world. Anatolia – Greece and Macedonia – had been subjugated by the Romans 300 years earlier after literally being on top of the heap. This was also the case for most of Asia Minor and Egypt, although generally their civilizations predated the Macedonian successes of Alexander the great. For much of northern Europe the Roman occupiers provided a level of civilization that exceeded that of most of the politically unstable tribal nation states that they had conquered.

At the same time the Roman power base was disintegrating from within, when Rome was in an expansionary phase of conquest there were many new challenges and opportunities, but now that it was the dominant power base throughout the then civilized world it became an army of policemen rather than of conquest. The power elite were more concerned with amusing themselves and satisfying their lust for pleasure than they were with moving their culture forward. With no more foreign conquests to swell the treasury in Rome the cost of maintaining this extensive police force was almost unmanageable, and the conquered people were labouring under an oppressive level of taxation. The common people of Rome were not treated much better.

The Roman overlords took no interest in the religious beliefs of conquered peoples, and allowed them to continue their practices as long as it did not interfere with Roman self interest. As noted earlier, they were very happy with the already established taxation system that existed in the kingdoms of Israel and left the religious affairs in the hands of the Temple leaders. Aside from the monotheistic Hebrew faith that was based in Jerusalem all of the other pagan cultures worshiped idols and false gods, none of which ever provided any relief or personal comfort that could equal that provided by the new sect of the Judaic faith. The conquered people were disenchanted and despairing, ready to embrace any faith that provided them with more than they were getting from their empty idols, they were ready for a message of hope.

Hope was the product that seized the imagination of the people, first the Jews but not too much later the people of every culture within the known world were scrambling to join the people of The Way. This raises another very interesting question, did these converts understand that Jesus taught that heaven and hell were here on earth, or were they buying into the concept that heaven was available only in the afterlife? At some point between the execution of Jesus and Mark's Gospel written 40 years later, the idea of an out of this world heaven surfaced, and became equated with Jesus and his message. How many times do you have to repeat something before it becomes an accepted truth? Matthew and Luke built much of their Gospels from the work that Mark had done, repeating the error and shamelessly embellishing the story until it looks like a scene from a movie.

How did this happen? In the Hebrew Scriptures thrones are very important, especially the throne of David, and proximity to the throne is a clear indication of approval and power. The prophets spoke of God sitting on his throne because that was the ultimate compliment they could give considering their limited worldview consisted of Judea and its neighbouring states. Inserting that Judaic vision into the picture that Jesus was trying to make clear made the whole concept of being saved by faith very easily understood by the masses of followers; something that is perfectly understandable but for which there is no basis in the teachings and actions of Jesus. Nevertheless, this appears to have become a fundamental part of the belief system for followers of The Way, without it how many of them would have offered themselves gladly to die for their faith?

And that brings us to the second part of the question, how did this Middle Eastern phenomena become a major formative factor in the world? This fast growing religion was decimating the ranks of the plethora of pagan cultures with its message of hope and salvation, people could not get enough of it! By the end of the third century even Rome had come to that conclusion and Emperor Constantine converted to Christianity early in the fourth century. It is possible, but seriously doubtful, that his motivation was completely spiritual. His actions put him in the position of effectively controlling the entire Roman Empire without maintaining an expensive army. It was Constantine who build St. Peter's Basilica and formally established the papacy, setting the wheels in motion for the development of a mega monarchy that transcended borders and played a pivotal political role in the development of Western civilization.

Was Jesus Really the Son of God?

While there is no question that Jesus believed himself to be the Son of God we have to ask ourselves if that was true. Jesus' belief was so strong and his charismatic power so influential that he was easily able to lead others to come to that conclusion. Mind you, the audience was anxiously awaiting the Messiah, they had been waiting for five centuries and it really took very little convincing to have them jump to that conclusion. In that respect he was really no different than other charismatic leaders the world has seen, but there were also several striking differences.

Firstly, he was able to perform miracles. These are well documented by numerous sources and his success at developing a substantial following was undeniably a direct result of possessing this supernatural power. While this by itself certainly was an incredible and unexplainable feat, what was even more remarkable was his ability to imbue his disciples with these powers, again something that is documented in several sources. We also have an interesting situation recorded in Matthew about another believer casting out demons and healing people in the name of Jesus of Nazareth, Jesus' response was that anyone who does this in his name does it with the blessing of God. Lastly, we have the resurrection, once again something that is very well documented in many reliable and independent sources. The greatest verification about the authenticity of the resurrection is provided by the events of history, this sole distinguishing feature was arguably the single deciding factor that spread the faith across the face of the known world within a century. It did in fact change the world.

The foregoing provides a very plausible basis for Jesus being the Son of God, but there are a number of other questions that come up. Jesus of Nazareth was a human being and a product of his socioeconomic background, otherwise he would have had a much broader worldview than he demonstrated as a member of the Hebrew faith in ancient Judea. If at some point he became the Son of God, he should have had a much different and significantly greater understanding because presumably he would have been exposed to the secrets of the all powerful God. Where is that demonstrated? Even after the resurrection, when he interacted with Paul on the road to Damascus, his instructions were still focused on a relatively small part of the world that we today refer to as the Middle East. The focus that the man Jesus had was clearly targeted at reinvigorating the Hebrew culture, the risen Jesus, the Son of God, broadened his view to include conversion of the Gentiles and expansion to the known world of antiquity. If he was the Son of God would he not have more information about the entire world and the workings of the cosmos that should exceed the understanding that we have gained through science in the 21st century?

The miraculous powers that Jesus possessed did not continue beyond the first generation of his faithful followers, why is that? While that does not in any way negate the importance of his miraculous works, one might well wonder why he abandoned the project after a few short years as the Holy Spirit. If he was the Son of God where has he been for the last two millennia when the movement founded in his name went so seriously wrong, and contributed to some of the worst atrocities recorded in history?

Jesus spoke of the coming of the end of times when judgment would be made by God as if it was imminent, so imminent that people stopped living normal lives in anticipation of the coming day of judgment. They disposed of their assets and donated everything to the cause, lived communally and spent their time ministering to the poor. This experiment in what we today would call communism was fairly short lived and within a few years people had reverted to their normal lifestyle, although their lives were not centred on the synagogue but around the system of churches that Paul initiated. The prophesied end of times never came and it eludes us still, apparently the man Jesus of Nazareth was mistaken and the risen Son of God did not see fit to correct the oversight.

So was Jesus actually the Son of God? While it is largely a matter of faith the facts speak much louder than words, and the facts recorded by history make it clear that something incredibly miraculous happened. No one has ever been able to explain this remarkable event, so the only logical conclusion we can arrive at is that it happened and it was real. Does that mean that Jesus was the Son of God? There really is no concrete answer to that question, perhaps the larger question is does it really matter anyway?

Jesus provided us with a code of conduct, reinforced the Golden Rule that we should treat other people the way we want to be treated, and he did set the world on fire with his message. Think about it, our entire Western culture has been shaped by the teachings of this brilliant prophet from Nazareth, and the faith communities that had been founded in his name. Our years are counted from the estimated year of the birth of Jesus. Whether we choose to believe that Jesus was the Son of God or not is a very personal matter of faith that is largely irrelevant in our role as inhabitants of the 21st century.

Who are impacted by this answer anyway? Does it make a difference of the world? No. Does it make a difference to the faithful? Yes. Does it make a difference to the masses who are not part of the Christian faith? No. Does it matter to the established churches? Yes, and no. Does it matter to you? As far as I am concerned it is irrelevant, the teachings are what matter.

What Matters to Christians Today?

Before we consider this question we must first come to some agreement about what it takes to be a Christian. Perhaps before that we should look at the validity of the Christian faith as it evolved following the apocalyptic year 70 CE, how does it compare to the true teachings of Jesus? Jesus did not create a new religion, his stated purpose was to get the Hebrew nation back on track and, early in his ministry, he specifically instructed his disciples to not approach the Gentiles and Sadducees. Paul was the creator and real father of the Christian church, it was his encounter with the risen Jesus on the road to Damascus and unrelenting commitment that democratized the faith and opened the door to people who were not practising Jews.

In the first century followers of The Way, people we today refer to as the first Christians, had a level of commitment that extended beyond their homes and communities, and were prepared to put their lives on the line for their faith. However, we must remember that these people were convinced that the end of times was imminent and they were going to join Jesus in heaven. In the 21st century there are a number of Christians who have committed themselves to serve their faith but it is very doubtful that the vast majority of those who call themselves Christian would willingly give up their lives for the cause.

Are we truly followers of the faith stream that began with Jesus of Nazareth, or are we adherents of a secularized, sanitized interpretation of the core message that better reflects our self interest and intention to survive at all costs? The entire Christian community as it exists today is a direct product of over 2000 years of bloodshed, conspiracy and duplicity inspired by greed and power, and would not in any way resonate with the members of the first century Jesus Movement. Why are we surprised when the majority of the people in our culture who come from a Christian background discard the core message and become token Christians?

Ostensibly we live in a Christian world, but our fundamental moral code is based on a selection of convenient Christian ethics as they have evolved over 2000 years. This diluted, homogenized version of the core message delivered by the man from Galilee does not make us a Christian culture, but it has turned us into a society that is by and large based on humanitarian principles. We go through the charade of following Christian values but cherry pick those that appeal to us and, using our intellect, develop a code of conduct that is more humanistic than anything else. Is that a problem? I think not, perhaps it is time that we shook off this oppressive yoke of guilt and obligation that has been grinding people down for 2000 years and get back to our roots. Look to the followers of The Way, read the words of Jesus and consider his actions as you deliberately choose your path into the future.

The Way Ahead

One does not need a crystal ball to foresee that the decline in the numbers of active Christians in the past 50 years will continue for the most part, resulting in many well established denominations shrinking or simply fading away. Their constituents will consist of aging parishioners who are clinging hopefully to long discredited ideas as they wait for God.

The more evangelical churches will do significantly better because they will be offering a true sense of Christian community in a dynamic environment that will appeal to younger people and families. The original Western church, what is now known as the Roman Catholic Church, will also be severely challenged in North America, but globally do much better than the mainstream Protestant denominations because of its ability to leverage its strong support in South America. The simplest way to gauge the success of any of the North American churches is to look at their seminaries, how many graduates are being inducted each year and how does that compare to 20 years ago? Is it any wonder that the North American Roman Catholic pulpits are being filled by priests from South America?

The concept of community envisioned by Jesus would not work in the first century that was driven by self interest and power, and it simply will not work in a 21st century society that is driven by our feeling of entitlement and our need for instant gratification. For those people prone to introspection, those of us who are looking for meaning beyond what we can see and feel, it will be very difficult to find communities of like minded people. When we do find them we need to embrace them and celebrate what we have found, because we will then have discovered the essence of what Jesus taught. This will not be a world of ritual, liturgy and sacred music, but it will be a community of humanness where people can acknowledge the existence of some power that they can never fully understand or know, and do everything in their power to create a life that is heaven on earth. As for the rest of the so called Christian world's population we cannot worry about them, as Jesus said "Let those who have ears to hear, hear."

Your Challenge

We are all accidental tourists in this experience of life, through no choice of our own, we just woke up here. The challenge we all face is making this incredible gift called life as fulfilling and rewarding as it possibly can be before we face the inevitability of bodily death.

The world has several major faiths with thousands of subgroups which have differing views about what happens when we die, but it really does not matter whether we identify with one of these faith streams or not. We do not need to stand behind a particular creed, that is just a label, it is not what defines us as human beings with a living soul. What we publicly profess is far less important than the way we demonstrate our beliefs through our lives.

Regardless of our personal and very individual belief system, every one of us is going to experience a physical death, are you ready for it? You need to take your own investigative journey and examine your soul and see if you like what you see, if you are not happy with what you find you still have time to change things and be the person you want to be for the rest of your life.

8 - The 21st Century Way to Life

Before we consider how The Way fits into our so very different 21st century, we first need to address the question of whether the teachings of a prophet who lived more than 2000 years ago have any relevance to the dynamic society we live in today. Does the message of Jesus fit? For many people it does not, and these are the majority of the population who have discarded organized religion as irrelevant to their lives and, more often than not, their decision is accurate. But we are not concerned with the masses here, even when the population was much smaller 2000 years ago we were cautioned to forget about those who would not hear. The willing acceptance of a state of blissful ignorance by the overwhelming majority has been with us as long as humans have walked this earth, and will continue until the end of time.

The major unintended but not unexpected finding of this study is the determination that people today are no different from the people of 2000, 4000 or 10,000 years ago; we are all driven by an instinctive urge to survive, live in community, raise our families and protect them at all costs. From the beginning of time we have had natural leaders emerge from obscure sources, as well as people with a commitment to hard work, while at the same time there were always those who preferred to take the easy road. There have always been those who are consumed by the questions of why and why not, and Jesus just happened to be one of those people who was in the right place at the right time with the right message. Much of what he taught can also be found in many ancient cultures and religions that were totally disconnected with the ancient world in which Jesus lived, they are universal truths that apply to every human being. So yes, the teachings of a rabbi who died 2000 years ago are very relevant to people today.

The Time Before Now

By the end of the first century, that is 30 years after the time that we have studied, the new faith that evolved into a dynamic force that spread across the world of antiquity and impacted every culture it touched. This was the time when all the synoptic Gospels and the Acts of the Apostles were written, while persecution of the followers of The Way was still an on again and off again affair. Eventually this would result in the first major schism in the church, between Western Catholicism and Eastern Orthodoxy, based in Rome and Constantinople respectively. The third branch of Christianity, based in Africa, died a natural death as the Moslem faith grew into prominence.

Within this increasingly complex structure, the Western church based in Rome, interpretive theology was being developed that, when viewed retrospectively, seems to have had more to do with structuring an organization that was secure and manageable than it did with following the core message of the teachings of Jesus. A plethora of manuscripts appeared in the second and third centuries claiming to be Gospels of one sort or another, and the rapidly developing church had a major responsibility to sort the genuine from the bogus, a monumental and very difficult task. It was from this work, that continued to the end of the third century, that the Bible was constructed with the contents that we see in it today. All of the contentious issues were finally resolved by decree at the Council of Nicaea in 325 CE, that is the official birthdate of the Bible as we know it.

In 312 CE the Roman Emperor Constantine converted to Christianity, immediately giving credibility to the faith across the Roman Empire. It was Constantine who supported the establishment of the Bishop of Rome in a pre-eminent role, enshrining the reign of popes and the papacy. It was he who constructed St. Peter's Basilica and had the bones of Peter reinterred there, creating a physical centre for a church that no longer needed to hide from the authorities.

With his conversion the entire Roman Empire was expected to convert to the new religion, which was a very complex problem because previously the Romans had been content to let conquered populations retain their own religions as long as they did not interfere with their allegiance to Rome. The church had taken two centuries to determine what was the right theology and what was heresy, and the now much mightier church, which referred to itself as the 'one true faith ', proceeded to root out heresy wherever it was to be found. The policies first articulated by the Bishop of Lyon, Irenaeus, in the later years of the second century and expanded by subsequent theologians, provided the justification for forced conversion or annihilation of the heretics. This continued well past the 16th century Spanish Inquisition and remnants of this decidedly unchristian behaviour continue to this day.

From its earliest beginnings the church had relied on oral transmission of information as the primary way of communicating with its congregants. This was consistent with the times, written documentation was scarce, extremely valuable and jealously protected by the small percentage of the population who were literate. There was no literacy requirement for the congregational leaders, they had no books to read anyway. This situation continued for several centuries, frequently the priests sent out to minister to congregations were functionally illiterate. The church members were given several visual tools to assist them in following their obligations of the faith, such as crucifixes, statues, paintings, the stations of the cross, the rosary and countless rituals that eliminated the need for literacy and the written word.

The actions of Martin Luther in 1517 CE initiated the second major fissure in the Western church, ultimately giving rise to the split between orthodox Christians who remained loyal to the Roman Catholic Church and the Protestants. While the Catholic Church remained relatively intact, secure in its structure that had stood the test of time, the Protestant churches continued to fracture and splinter. Special interest groups took hold of this opportunity to operate without the heavy handed governance from Rome, frequently led by monarchs intent on establishing their own national churches of which they could be the head, such as the Church of England under Henry VIII. Other denominations developed along nationalist lines, probably as much a result of language barriers as anything else; German Lutherans, Dutch Calvinists and so on.

In the middle of the 15th century the printing press was invented in Germany, and by the early 16th century it had been developed to the point where books could be produced in quantity. Until this time Bibles were not available to anyone except scholars and priests, so the Bible became the first book that was printed for commercial purposes, the demand was incredible. By this time literacy was expanding quickly, and well educated Europeans who generally had the ability to speak two or three languages rapidly embraced this new development.

217

Very soon Bibles were available to the common people in their own language, which rapidly fueled the growth of literacy and, for the first time, individuals were able to interpret the biblical teachings on their own without having to rely on the priests or church leaders for instruction in the faith. This had a very significant impact on the development of the Protestant churches, where people were now empowered to develop their own personal relationship with God.

The 19th century saw a proliferation of new Protestant permutations in the English speaking world, creating the Methodist and Presbyterian mainstream churches and a very broad spectrum in the evangelical churches. By the 20th century Christianity came in so many flavours that everyone could find a pew where they felt comfortable. The Roman Catholic Church served those who wanted ritual and stability, Anglican and Episcopalian churches satisfied those who wanted something structured but a little more democratic, while those who needed something with a looser structure moved to the Methodist, Presbyterian, United and Baptist denominations. The evangelical churches were even more responsive to people's needs and discarded much of the ritual and liturgy in favour of a more contemporary approach that had a much broader appeal. In spite of all of this choice there were still great hordes of people who opted out, content to live in a society defined by Christian values but wanting no part in any celebration of faith.

What Does Now Look Like?

The 21st century Western world is better defined by its gadgets and gizmos that it is by any ideology. Information that was once available only to a few is now available to everyone, in far greater abundance than anyone can cope with or requires. In centuries past, and even today, the activities of simple survival often require a full time commitment. Nevertheless, in our 21st century society there are many people with more time available to do things they choose to do rather than spending all their time working to stay alive. Leisure time activities have become a major driving force in every Western country's economy, ensuring that everyone is too busy with their optional activities of choice to give much thought to the spiritual aspect of their lives. Ironically, as people approach the end of their lives they begin to think of such things, but is it not too late? Does end of life repentance actually compensate for a spiritually empty life of self indulgence?

The Relevance of Faith

In the almost four decades that I have been living with a progressive disease there have been many times when I have been asked to speak with people whose lives have been touched by multiple sclerosis, to help them understand how it will impact their lives and their personal relationships. It quickly became apparent that there was a significant difference in how a person of faith would deal with this calamity, as compared to someone with no faith. In general, the person of faith was better equipped to come to terms with this very unwelcome new reality in their life. Skeptics will quickly point out that the presence of faith in the equation simply provides the believer with false hope, but if that hope allows a person to get on with their life and make the most of a difficult situation, is this not better than living without any hope? Equating faith with hope creates a very powerful formula for living a positive and fulfilling life.

Hope is a very important, but unfortunately, a very scarce commodity across the world. Every culture rapidly embraces positive stories of hopefulness in situations that on the surface appear to be quite hopeless. Whether it is in the news, popular literature and magazines, television, movies or in places of worship of every faith, hope is the common denominator, the great leveler. It really does not seem to matter what the basis for your faith/hope is, but a life without hope must be incredibly hard to live. Nowhere is this more evident than in our medical systems. People who have no will to live will simply not cope well when stricken by a serious disease, while people of faith who are looking forward to living have a better chance of recovery.

Those people who live with faith are decidedly better able to cope with the traumas of living than those who live without faith, but does it matter what you have faith in? Is the simple fact that one has faith in something that is greater than themselves and beyond their understanding what is really important, and the details are insignificant? Does it really matter if you are Buddhist, Christian, Hindu, Muslim or a myriad of other faith streams? I do not think it matters at all, the path each of us follows has more to do with the culture in which we had been raised and our individual comfort level. There is no incontrovertible evidence to the contrary, what you believe is less important than the fact that you have some belief system that provides you with comfort and hope. This reality certainly makes a mockery of all the strife the world continues to endure in the name of religion.

Our Need for Community

Human beings are communal creatures and have been since the beginning of time, this is so self evident it hardly warrants anything more than a mention. We cluster in groups where we feel comfortable. There are innumerable potential venues where we can develop relationships and foster our personal need to be part of a community. Most of us are members of several groups that may or may not overlap, and sometimes may appear to be conflicting, but that is as it should be because each of us needs to develop broadly to satisfy our unique and intensely personal interests. Participation in communities allows us to express our individual personalities in a safe and congenial environment.

The importance of community was empirically tested by a French sociologist, in 1879 Emile Durkheim studied the rate of suicides between Roman Catholic and Protestant populations. In the 19th century Roman Catholics followed a very diligent pattern of practicing their faith while the breakaway Protestant groups were continually fracturing and losing their sense of community. The Protestants won this contest hands down, the Roman Catholic community had a unity of purpose and commonality of faith that significantly reduced the rate of suicide in their ranks. Both the Roman Catholic and Protestant populations would have proportionately had the same causes for despair and extreme anxiety, so why was the Protestant suicide rate so much higher? Durkheim concluded that it was attributable to the more intense feeling of belonging to a solid and unshakable community that the Roman Catholic populations enjoyed.

Communities of the faithful were intensely important to the followers of The Way, a structure that was directly supported by the teachings of Jesus. What does this mean for our modern society where the communities of faith are in decline while the communities of shared interests are rising quickly? Can these secular communities provide enough fuel for the human spirit to satisfy our need for meaning? Apparently the answer is yes for some people, but not all.

What about the need that some of us have for faith in a power greater than ourselves, a need that pre-modern human beings have always had? Obviously not, so what do we do? We live in an age when young people are searching for some person or cause in which they can place their hope, they are searching for faith in something, but they cannot define what that something is, and it is very likely that they do not even realize the search is underway. The technological revolution that took off in the 80s has created an entirely new way of communicating that will undoubtedly fuel the development of some future pattern of hope, building a community of faith that fills the void. What will that look like?

What does this mean for our current structure of established churches in the Western world and especially North America? Many will fail, pastors, ministers, priests and congregations will finally tire of devoting all their time, energy and resources to maintaining buildings that are never fully utilized. The faithful will continue to be demoralized as their ranks thin at a rate that is far greater than the rate of repletion from the influx of new members. Only those churches that provide congregants with a strong feeling of community will survive and thrive. They will attract young people and their families, providing a vibrant life experience in a Christian setting that will be very similar to the one I enjoyed 50 years ago.

Following The Way in the 21st Century

The first two chapters of the first century document that was later known as the Didache are remarkably congruent with our Western standards that dictate decent behaviour. Is that an indication of the huge impact that the Christian faith made on the world, reflecting the adoption of Christian values as Western societies and cultures evolved? The answer is yes but, with a major qualifier.

Many of the rules for living set out in chapters 1 and 2 predate the time of Jesus by at least two millennia. Jewish history credits Moses with being given the ten commandments by God, all of which are included in the requirements for followers of

The Way. Every ancient civilization contained similar provisions about behaviour within the tribe. Is it coincidence that every major religion has the equivalent of the Golden Rule as part of its faith? No, but the reason has nothing to do with religion and everything to do with how civilization developed in communities of people with common interests. They needed rules to live by so they could enjoy a sense of security and function as a community rather than as a collection of individuals that did not have anything in common.

Jesus did set the world on fire with his message and his teachings, which solidified and further refined the definition of the right way to live. In half a century his followers, the followers of The Way, managed to have a far greater impact on the development of a definition of civilized behaviour than had been accomplished in the preceding 20 centuries. Their biggest, albeit undoubtedly unintended, contribution was recognizing that teachings of the past were of immense value, and they could be built on by introducing new ideas and concepts, thereby creating a better society. This did not simply result because of the actual teachings of Jesus, it was propelled by the unique and totally unexplainable event of his resurrection. Without the firepower provided by that supernatural event Christianity would never have become the unifying and often terrifying force that drove it from 30 CE for the next 2000 years.

During the 20th century the definition of civilized behaviour began to change rapidly, evolving to develop an ethical code that addressed atrocities that, in the past, would have been unknown to the world. As we moved into the technological age we developed much more efficient ways of committing atrocities, but at the same time advances in communication meant that everything became public. In this second decade of the 21st century our ability for instantaneous transmission means that the time lapse between the occurrence of events and public awareness is a matter of minutes. This has increased our global sensitivities to an extent that we are modifying the definition of acceptable behaviour as events unfold.

If we are to follow The Way in the 21st century we need to reflect these realities. We need to expand the list to encompass the much broader world view that we live with each day. People who wish to follow

The Way of Life in the 21st century and beyond will have to make a conscious decision about what they believe is the right path, and then live their lives in accordance with their beliefs. In short, they need to follow the Quakers' advice and 'listen to the wee small voice within' so they can find their unique faith within themselves.

Rules of behaviour emerged in every civilization throughout antiquity to establish what was acceptable behaviour within the community, thereby providing a harmonious and relatively safe living environment where internal strife was minimized. The Judaic community was heavily focused on faith in the presence of an invisible, terrifying God so the commandments as delivered by Moses served to reinforce that faith. It is very likely that the Judaic community was following these rules for living long before they were enshrined in their religious history when Moses went up the mountain.

The framework provided by the 10 Commandments was expanded very significantly by Hebrew scholars of 4000 years ago with several hundred rules of behaviour that were to be followed by members of the Jewish community. From our modern point of view this created a severely restrictive society, but it served its purpose very well; Judaism is the only faith of antiquity that has survived to the 21st century. The Jewish religion and culture has remained intact for at least four millennia in the face of overwhelming odds, and continues to thrive. Belonging to a close knit community that was held together by the glue of faith was a successful prescription for survival that no other ancient culture enjoyed.

By comparison to the very specific ten commandments delivered by Moses the additional standards for behaviour that developed from the teachings of Jesus are rather complex and fairly detailed. They also reflect the social realities that existed in the first century, which means that they may not be particularly relevant to today, although that is a matter of personal choice. To facilitate a meaningful review these added first century teachings for those who followed The Way have been grouped together by subject area.

Conflict

Bless those who curse you and pray for your enemies.
Love those who hate you.

If someone strikes your right cheek, turn to him the other also, if someone requires you go for one mile, go with him two. If someone takes your cloak, give him also your coat.

If someone takes from you what is yours, do not ask for it back.

Personal Relationships

Love your neighbour as yourself.

Treat other people the way you want to be treated.

Charity

Give to everyone who asks and expect nothing in return, give of your own free will.

Only accept help if you need it.

Be not a stretcher forth of the hands to receive and a drawer of them back to give.

Do not hesitate to give, nor complain when you give.

Do not turn away from him who is in want; rather, share all things with your brother, and do not say that they are your own.

Let your money sweat in your hands until you know to whom it should be given.

The Occult

Do not practice magic or witchcraft.

Be not an observer of omens.

Be neither an enchanter, nor an astrologer, nor a purifier, nor be willing to look at these things.

Family

Do not remove your hand from your son or daughter; rather, teach them the fear of God from their youth.

Do not murder a child by abortion nor kill that which is born.

Personal Behaviour

Do not swear.

Do not speak evil.

Bear no grudge.

You shall not be double-minded nor double-tongued.

Your speech shall not be false, nor empty, but fulfilled by deed.

You shall not be covetous, nor greedy, nor a hypocrite, nor evil disposed, nor haughty.

You shall not take evil counsel against your neighbour.

Do not hate any man; but some you shall reprove, and concerning some you shall pray, and some you shall love more than your own life.

Flee from every evil thing, and from every likeness of it.

Be not prone to anger.

Be neither jealous, nor quarrelsome, nor of hot temper.

Be neither a filthy talker, nor of lofty eye.

Be neither money-loving, nor vainglorious.

Do not long for division, but rather bring those who contend to peace.

Judge righteously, and do not respect persons in reproving for transgressions. You shall not be undecided whether or not it shall be.

Sexual Issues

Abstain from fleshly and worldly lusts.

You shall not commit pederasty.

Do not commit fornication (sex without being married).

These rules for living were carried into the developing church and incorporated in the ever increasing body of dogma, ritual and liturgy that has grown exponentially over the past 2000 years. That does not mean that this original code of conduct was followed by people that called themselves Christians or the Christian churches, the self proclaimed keepers of the faith, something that has not substantially changed to this day. I seriously doubt that there is anyone living or dead who could adhere to all of these life guidelines, and that is where the concept of sin comes into play. We are all sinners but the question is how much sinning is acceptable? And in your personal faith journey, do you have your own parameters for sin?

In the 19th and 20th centuries the world experienced incredible atrocities and the means to communicate those realities broadly and rapidly. This culminated in the wholesale adoption of several new concepts that are ingrained in the mindset of the 21st century Western world and must be taken into account by today's followers of The Way of Life. These deal with:

Genocide
Human Rights
Paedophilia
Gender equality
Abolition of slavery

These ideals, like those from antiquity and the first century, indicate the direction in which modern people and societies should move if they want to live a life that is consistent with the teachings of Jesus and the early Christian tradition. In the 21st century we will undoubtedly see the list of acceptable behaviour expanded and fine tuned as humanity addresses some major questions such as religious intolerance and the distribution of resources.

Mapping Your Own Journey

This journey began because I was uncomfortable with what I was being told while sitting in the pew, and I decided to get to the root cause of my discomfort. I have done that and you have read my findings, I have not given up hope nor have I lost my faith. My understanding of who I am and where I fit in the cosmos is greater, that I have this wonderful thing called life proves to me that I am an infinitesimal but integral part of the unfathomable everything. I know that I have a soul, the part of me that contains the divine spark of life that makes me who I am. My faith has changed for the better because it is grounded in what I know, or more precisely in what I can never know or understand, and not in what I have been told. Now it is time for you to undertake your own journey.

Appendices

1 - The Gospel of Thomas

This work contains 114 sayings of Jesus that were written down at the time they were spoken and undoubtedly formed part of the body of information that was available to the first and second generation Christians. Thomas was a disciple and this was found with the discovery of the Dead Sea Scrolls in 1956.

The Gospel of Thomas

Translated by Thomas O. Lambdin

Selection made from James M. Robinson, ed.,
The Nag
Hammadi   Library,   revised   edition.
HarperCollins, 1990

These are the secret sayings which the living Jesus spoke and which Didymos Judas Thomas wrote down.

(1) And he said, "Whoever finds the interpretation of these sayings will not experience death."

(2) Jesus said, "Let him who seeks continue seeking until he finds. When he finds, he

will become troubled. When he becomes troubled, he will be astonished, and he will rule over the All."

(3) Jesus said, "If those who lead you say to you, 'See, the kingdom is in the sky,' then the birds of the sky will precede you. If they say to you, 'It is in the sea,' then the fish will precede you. Rather, the kingdom is inside of you, and it is outside of you. When you come to know yourselves, then you will become known, and you will realize that it is you who are the sons of the living father. But if you will not know yourselves, you dwell in poverty and it is you who are that poverty."

(4) Jesus said, "The man old in days will not hesitate to ask a small child seven days old about the place of life, and he will live. For many who are first will become last, and they will become one and the same."

(5) Jesus said, "Recognize what is in your sight, and that which is hidden from you will become plain to you. For there is nothing hidden which will not become manifest."

(6) His disciples questioned him and said to him, "Do you want us to fast? How shall we pray? Shall we give alms? What diet shall we observe?"

Jesus said, "Do not tell lies, and do not do what you hate, for all things are plain in the sight of heaven. For nothing hidden will not become manifest, and nothing covered will remain without being uncovered."

(7) Jesus said, "Blessed is the lion which becomes man when consumed by man; and cursed is the man whom the lion consumes, and the lion becomes man."

(8) And he said, "The man is like a wise fisherman who cast his net into the sea and drew it up from the sea full of small fish. Among them the wise fisherman found a fine large fish. He threw all the small fish back into the sea and chose the large fish without difficulty. Whoever has ears to hear, let him hear."

(9) Jesus said, "Now the sower went out, took a handful (of seeds), and scattered them. Some fell on the road; the birds came and gathered them up. Others fell on the rock, did not take root in the soil, and did not produce ears. And others fell on thorns; they choked the seed(s) and worms ate them. And others fell on the good soil and it produced good fruit: it bore sixty per measure and a hundred and twenty per measure."

(10) Jesus said, "I have cast fire upon the world, and see, I am guarding it until it blazes."

(11) Jesus said, "This heaven will pass away, and the one above it will pass away. The dead are not alive, and the living will not die. In the days when you consumed what is dead, you made it what is alive. When you come to dwell in the light, what will you do? On the day when you were one you became two. But when you become two, what will you do?"

(12) The disciples said to Jesus, "We know that you will depart from us. Who is to be our leader?"
Jesus said to them, "Wherever you are, you are to go to James the righteous, for whose sake heaven and earth came into being."

(13) Jesus said to his disciples, "Compare me to someone and tell me whom I am like."
Simon Peter said to him, "You are like a righteous angel."
Matthew said to him, "You are like a wise philosopher."
Thomas said to him, "Master, my mouth is wholly incapable of saying whom you are like."
Jesus said, "I am not your master. Because

*you have drunk, you have become
intoxicated from the bubbling spring which I
have measured out."*

*And he took him and withdrew and told him
three things. When Thomas returned to his
companions, they asked him, "What did
Jesus say to you?"*

*Thomas said to them, "If I tell you one of
the things which he told me, you will pick up
stones and throw them at me; a fire will
come out of the stones and burn you up."*

*(14) Jesus said to them, "If you fast, you will
give rise to sin for yourselves; and if you
pray, you will be condemned; and if you
give alms, you will do harm to your spirits.
When you go into any land and walk about
in the districts, if they receive you, eat what
they will set before you, and heal the sick
among them. For what goes into your
mouth will not defile you, but that which
issues from your mouth - it is that which will
defile you."*

*(15) Jesus said, "When you see one who
was not born of woman, prostrate
yourselves on your faces and worship him.
That one is your father."*

*(16) Jesus said, "Men think, perhaps, that it
is peace which I have come to cast upon
the world. They do not know that it is*

dissension which I have come to cast upon the earth: fire, sword, and war. For there will be five in a house: three will be against two, and two against three, the father against the son, and the son against the father. And they will stand solitary."

(17) Jesus said, "I shall give you what no eye has seen and what no ear has heard and what no hand has touched and what has never occurred to the human mind."

(18) The disciples said to Jesus, "Tell us how our end will be."
Jesus said, "Have you discovered, then, the beginning, that you look for the end? For where the beginning is, there will the end be. Blessed is he who will take his place in the beginning; he will know the end and will not experience death."

(19) Jesus said, "Blessed is he who came into being before he came into being. If you become my disciples and listen to my words, these stones will minister to you. For there are five trees for you in Paradise which remain undisturbed summer and winter and whose leaves do not fall. Whoever becomes acquainted with them will not experience death."

(20) The disciples said to Jesus, "Tell us what the kingdom of heaven is like." He said to them, "It is like a mustard seed. It is the smallest of all seeds. But when it falls on tilled soil, it produces a great plant and becomes a shelter for birds of the sky."

(21) Mary said to Jesus, "Whom are your disciples like?"
He said, "They are like children who have settled in a field which is not theirs. When the owners of the field come, they will say, 'Let us have back our field.' They (will) undress in their presence in order to let them have back their field and to give it back to them. Therefore I say, if the owner of a house knows that the thief is coming, he will begin his vigil before he comes and will not let him dig through into his house of his domain to carry away his goods. You, then, be on your guard against the world. Arm yourselves with great strength lest the robbers find a way to come to you, for the difficulty which you expect will (surely) materialize. Let there be among you a man of understanding. When the grain ripened, he came quickly with his sickle in his hand and reaped it. Whoever has ears to hear, let him hear."

(22) Jesus saw infants being suckled. He said to his disciples, "These infants being

suckled are like those who enter the
kingdom."
They said to him, "Shall we then, as
children, enter the kingdom?"
Jesus said to them, "When you make the
two one, and when you make the inside like
the outside and the outside like the inside,
and the above like the below, and when you
make the male and the female one and the
same, so that the male not be male nor the
female; and when you fashion eyes in the
place of an eye, and a hand in place of a
hand, and a foot in place of a foot, and a
likeness in place of a likeness; then will you
enter the kingdom."

(23) Jesus said, "I shall choose you, one
out of a thousand, and two out of ten
thousand, and they shall stand as a single
one."

(24) His disciples said to him, "Show us the
place where you are, since it is necessary
for us to seek it."
He said to them, "Whoever has ears, let
him hear. There is light within a man of
light, and he lights up the whole world. If he
does not shine, he is darkness."

(25) Jesus said, "Love your brother like
your soul, guard him like the pupil of your
eye."

(26) Jesus said, "You see the mote in your brother's eye, but you do not see the beam in your own eye. When you cast the beam out of your own eye, then you will see clearly to cast the mote from your brother's eye."

(27) Jesus said, "If you do not fast as regards the world, you will not find the kingdom. If you do not observe the Sabbath as a Sabbath, you will not see the father."

(28) Jesus said, "I took my place in the midst of the world, and I appeared to them in flesh. I found all of them intoxicated; I found none of them thirsty. And my soul became afflicted for the sons of men, because they are blind in their hearts and do not have sight; for empty they came into the world, and empty too they seek to leave the world. But for the moment they are intoxicated. When they shake off their wine, then they will repent."

(29) Jesus said, "If the flesh came into being because of spirit, it is a wonder. But if spirit came into being because of the body, it is a wonder of wonders. Indeed, I am amazed at how this great wealth has made its home in this poverty."

(30) Jesus said, "Where there are three gods, they are gods. Where there are two or one, I am with him."

(31) Jesus said, "No prophet is accepted in his own village; no physician heals those who know him."

(32) Jesus said, "A city being built on a high mountain and fortified cannot fall, nor can it be hidden."

(33) Jesus said, "Preach from your housetops that which you will hear in your ear. For no one lights a lamp and puts it under a bushel, nor does he put it in a hidden place, but rather he sets it on a lampstand so that everyone who enters and leaves will see its light."

(34) Jesus said, "If a blind man leads a blind man, they will both fall into a pit."

(35) Jesus said, "It is not possible for anyone to enter the house of a strong man and take it by force unless he binds his hands; then he will (be able to) ransack his house."

(36) Jesus said, "Do not be concerned from morning until evening and from evening until morning about what you will wear."

(37) His disciples said, "When will you become revealed to us and when shall we see you?"

Jesus said, "When you disrobe without being ashamed and take up your garments and place them under your feet like little children and tread on them, then will you see the son of the living one, and you will not be afraid"

(38) Jesus said, "Many times have you desired to hear these words which I am saying to you, and you have no one else to hear them from. There will be days when you will look for me and will not find me."

(39) Jesus said, "The Pharisees and the scribes have taken the keys of knowledge (gnosis) and hidden them. They themselves have not entered, nor have they allowed to enter those who wish to. You, however, be as wise as serpents and as innocent as doves."

(40) Jesus said, "A grapevine has been planted outside of the father, but being unsound, it will be pulled up by its roots and destroyed."

(41) Jesus said, "Whoever has something in his hand will receive more, and whoever

has nothing will be deprived of even the little he has."

(42) Jesus said, "Become passers-by."

(43) His disciples said to him, "Who are you, that you should say these things to us?"
Jesus said to them, "You do not realize who I am from what I say to you, but you have become like the Jews, for they (either) love the tree and hate its fruit (or) love the fruit and hate the tree."

(44) Jesus said, "Whoever blasphemes against the father will be forgiven, and whoever blasphemes against the son will be forgiven, but whoever blasphemes against the holy spirit will not be forgiven either on earth or in heaven."

(45) Jesus said, "Grapes are not harvested from thorns, nor are figs gathered from thistles, for they do not produce fruit. A good man brings forth good from his storehouse; an evil man brings forth evil things from his evil storehouse, which is in his heart, and says evil things. For out of the abundance of the heart he brings forth evil things."

(46) Jesus said, "Among those born of women, from Adam until John the Baptist, there is no one so superior to John the Baptist that his eyes should not be lowered (before him). Yet I have said, whichever one of you comes to be a child will be acquainted with the kingdom and will become superior to John."

(47) Jesus said, "It is impossible for a man to mount two horses or to stretch two bows. And it is impossible for a servant to serve two masters; otherwise, he will honour the one and treat the other contemptuously. No man drinks old wine and immediately desires to drink new wine. And new wine is not put into old wineskins, lest they burst; nor is old wine put into a new wineskin, lest it spoil it. An old patch is not sewn onto a new garment, because a tear would result."

(48) Jesus said, "If two make peace with each other in this one house, they will say to the mountain, 'Move Away,' and it will move away."

(49) Jesus said, "Blessed are the solitary and elect, for you will find the kingdom. For you are from it, and to it you will return."

(50) Jesus said, "If they say to you, 'Where did you come from?' say to them, 'we came

from the light, the place where the light came into being on its own accord and established itself and became manifest through their image.' If they say to you, 'is it you?' say, 'We are its children, we are the elect of the living father.' If they ask you, 'What is the sign of your father in you?' say to them, 'It is movement and repose.'"

(51) His disciples said to him, "When will the repose of the dead come about, and when will the new world come?"
He said to them, "What you look forward to has already come, but you do not recognize it."

(52) His disciples said to him, "Twenty-four prophets spoke in Israel, and all of them spoke in you."
He said to them, "You have omitted the one living in your presence and have spoken (only) of the dead."

(53) His disciples said to him, "Is circumcision beneficial or not?"
He said to them, "If it were beneficial, their father would beget them already circumcised from their mother. Rather, the true circumcision in spirit has become completely profitable."

(54) Jesus said, "Blessed are the poor, for yours is the kingdom of heaven."

(55) Jesus said, "Whoever does not hate his father and his mother cannot become a disciple to me. And whoever does not hate his brothers and sisters and take up his cross in my way will not be worthy of me."

(56) Jesus said, "Whoever has come to understand the world has found (only) a corpse, and whoever has found a corpse is superior to the world."

(57) Jesus said, "The kingdom of the father is like a man who had good seed. His enemy came by night and sowed weeds among the good seed. The man did not allow them to pull up the weeds; he said to them, 'I am afraid that you will go intending to pull up the weeds and pull up the wheat along with them.' For on the day of the harvest the weeds will be plainly visible, and they will be pulled up and burned."

(58) Jesus said, "Blessed is the man who has suffered and found life."

(59) Jesus said, "Take heed of the living one while you are alive, lest you die and seek to see him and be unable to do so."

(60) They saw a Samaritan carrying a lamb on his way to Judea. He said to his disciples, "That man is round about the lamb." They said to him, "So that he may kill it and eat it."

He said to them, "While it is alive, he will not eat it, but only when he has killed it and it has become a corpse."

They said to him, "He cannot do so otherwise."

He said to them, "You too, look for a place for yourself within repose, lest you become a corpse and be eaten."

(61) Jesus said, "Two will rest on a bed: the one will die, and the other will live."

Salome said, "Who are you, man, that you ... have come up on my couch and eaten from my table?"

Jesus said to her, "I am he who exists from the undivided. I was given some of the things of my father."

<...> "I am your disciple."

<...> "Therefore I say, if he is destroyed, he will be filled with light, but if he is divided, he will be filled with darkness."

(62) Jesus said, "It is to those who are worthy of my mysteries that I tell my mysteries. Do not let your left (hand) know what your right (hand) is doing."

(63) Jesus said, "There was a rich man who had much money. He said, 'I shall put my money to use so that I may sow, reap, plant, and fill my storehouse with produce, with the result that I shall lack nothing.' Such were his intentions, but that same night he died. Let him who has ears hear."

(64) Jesus said, "A man had received visitors. And when he had prepared the dinner, he sent his servant to invite the guests.

He went to the first one and said to him, 'My master invites you.' He said, 'I have claims against some merchants. They are coming to me this evening. I must go and give them my orders. I ask to be excused from the dinner.'

He went to another and said to him, 'My master has invited you.' He said to him, 'I have just bought a house and am required for the day. I shall not have any spare time.'

He went to another and said to him, 'My master invites you.' He said to him, 'My friend is going to get married, and I am to prepare the banquet. I shall not be able to come. I ask to be excused from the dinner.'

He went to another and said to him, 'My master invites you.' He said to him, 'I have just bought a farm, and I am on my way to collect the rent. I shall not be able to come. I ask to be excused.'

The servant returned and said to his master, 'Those whom you invited to the dinner have asked to be excused.' The master said to his servant, 'Go outside to the streets and bring back those whom you happen to meet, so that they may dine.' Businessmen and merchants will not enter the places of my father."

(65) He said, "There was a good man who owned a vineyard. He leased it to tenant farmers so that they might work it and he might collect the produce from them. He sent his servant so that the tenants might give him the produce of the vineyard. They seized his servant and beat him, all but killing him. The servant went back and told his master. The master said, 'Perhaps he did not recognize them.' He sent another servant. The tenants beat this one as well. Then the owner sent his son and said, 'Perhaps they will show respect to my son.' Because the tenants knew that it was he who was the heir to the vineyard, they seized him and killed him. Let him who has ears hear."

(66) Jesus said, "Show me the stone which the builders have rejected. That one is the cornerstone."

(67) Jesus said, "If one who knows the all still feels a personal deficiency, he is completely deficient."

(68) Jesus said, "Blessed are you when you are hated and persecuted. Wherever you have been persecuted they will find no place."

(69) Jesus said, "Blessed are they who have been persecuted within themselves. It is they who have truly come to know the father. Blessed are the hungry, for the belly of him who desires will be filled."

(70) Jesus said, "That which you have will save you if you bring it forth from yourselves. That which you do not have within you will kill you if you do not have it within you."

(71) Jesus said, "I shall destroy this house, and no one will be able to build it [...]."

(72) A man said to him, "Tell my brothers to divide my father's possessions with me."
He said to him, "O man, who has made me a divider?"

He turned to his disciples and said to them, "I am not a divider, am I?"

(73) Jesus said, "The harvest is great but the labourers are few. Beseech the Lord, therefore, to send out labourers to the harvest."

(74) He said, "O Lord, there are many around the drinking trough, but there is nothing in the cistern."

(75) Jesus said, "Many are standing at the door, but it is the solitary who will enter the bridal chamber."

(76) Jesus said, "The kingdom of the father is like a merchant who had a consignment of merchandise and who discovered a pearl. That merchant was shrewd. He sold the merchandise and bought the pearl alone for himself. You too, seek his unfailing and enduring treasure where no moth comes near to devour and no worm destroys."

(77) Jesus said, "It is I who am the light which is above them all. It is I who am the all. From me did the all come forth, and unto me did the all extend. Split a piece of wood, and I am there. Lift up the stone, and you will find me there."

(78) Jesus said, "Why have you come out into the desert? To see a reed shaken by the wind? And to see a man clothed in fine garments like your kings and your great men? Upon them are the fine garments, and they are unable to discern the truth."

(79) A woman from the crowd said to him, "Blessed are the womb which bore you and the breasts which nourished you."
He said to her, "Blessed are those who have heard the word of the father and have truly kept it. For there will be days when you will say, 'Blessed are the womb which has not conceived and the breasts which have not given milk.'"

(80) Jesus said, "He who has recognized the world has found the body, but he who has found the body is superior to the world."

(81) Jesus said, "Let him who has grown rich be king, and let him who possesses power renounce it."

(82) Jesus said, "He who is near me is near the fire, and he who is far from me is far from the kingdom."

(83) Jesus said, "The images are manifest to man, but the light in them remains concealed in the image of the light of the

father. He will become manifest, but his image will remain concealed by his light."

(84) Jesus said, "When you see your likeness, you rejoice. But when you see your images which came into being before you, and which neither die not become manifest, how much you will have to bear!"

(85) Jesus said, "Adam came into being from a great power and a great wealth, but he did not become worthy of you. For had he been worthy, he would not have experienced death."

(86) Jesus said, "The foxes have their holes and the birds have their nests, but the son of man has no place to lay his head and rest."

(87) Jesus said, "Wretched is the body that is dependent upon a body, and wretched is the soul that is dependent on these two."

(88) Jesus said, "The angels and the prophets will come to you and give to you those things you (already) have. And you too, give them those things which you have, and say to yourselves, 'When will they come and take what is theirs?'"

(89) Jesus said, "Why do you wash the outside of the cup? Do you not realize that he who made the inside is the same one who made the outside?"

(90) Jesus said, "Come unto me, for my yoke is easy and my lordship is mild, and you will find repose for yourselves."

(91) They said to him, "Tell us who you are so that we may believe in you."
He said to them, "You read the face of the sky and of the earth, but you have not recognized the one who is before you, and you do not know how to read this moment."

(92) Jesus said, "Seek and you will find. Yet, what you asked me about in former times and which I did not tell you then, now I do desire to tell, but you do not inquire after it."

(93) Jesus said, "Do not give what is holy to dogs, lest they throw them on the dung-heap. Do not throw the pearls to swine, lest they [...] it [...]."

(94) Jesus said, "He who seeks will find, and he who knocks will be let in."

(95) Jesus said, "If you have money, do not lend it at interest, but give it to one from whom you will not get it back."

(96) Jesus said, "The kingdom of the father is like a certain woman. She took a little leaven, concealed it in some dough, and made it into large loaves. Let him who has ears hear."

(97) Jesus said, "The kingdom of the father is like a certain woman who was carrying a jar full of meal. While she was walking on the road, still some distance from home, the handle of the jar broke and the meal emptied out behind her on the road. She did not realize it; she had noticed no accident. When she reached her house, she set the jar down and found it empty."

(98) Jesus said, "The kingdom of the father is like a certain man who wanted to kill a powerful man. In his own house he drew his sword and stuck it into the wall in order to find out whether his hand could carry through. Then he slew the powerful man."

(99) The disciples said to him, "Your brothers and your mother are standing outside."
He said to them, "Those here who do the will of my father are my brothers and my

mother. It is they who will enter the kingdom of my father."

(100) They showed Jesus a gold coin and said to him, "Caesar's men demand taxes from us."
He said to them, "Give Caesar what belongs to Caesar, give God what belongs to God, and give me what is mine."

(101) Jesus said, "Whoever does not hate his father and his mother as I do cannot become a disciple to me. And whoever does not love his father and his mother as I do cannot become a disciple to me. For my mother [...], but my true mother gave me life."

(102) Jesus said, "Woe to the Pharisees, for they are like a dog sleeping in the manger of oxen, for neither does he eat nor does he let the oxen eat."

(103) Jesus said, "Fortunate is the man who knows where the brigands will enter, so that he may get up, muster his domain, and arm himself before they invade."

(104) They said to Jesus, "Come, let us pray today and let us fast."

Jesus said, "What is the sin that I have committed, or wherein have I been defeated? But when the bridegroom leaves the bridal chamber, then let them fast and pray."

(105) Jesus said, "He who knows the father and the mother will be called the son of a harlot."

(106) Jesus said, "When you make the two one, you will become the sons of man, and when you say, 'Mountain, move away,' it will move away."

(107) Jesus said, "The kingdom is like a shepherd who had a hundred sheep. One of them, the largest, went astray. He left the ninety-nine sheep and looked for that one until he found it. When he had gone to such trouble, he said to the sheep, 'I care for you more than the ninety-nine.'"

(108) Jesus said, "He who will drink from my mouth will become like me. I myself shall become he, and the things that are hidden will be revealed to him."

(109) Jesus said, "The kingdom is like a man who had a hidden treasure in his field without knowing it. And after he died, he left it to his son. The son did not know (about

the treasure). He inherited the field and sold it. And the one who bought it went plowing and found the treasure. He began to lend money at interest to whomever he wished."

(110) Jesus said, "Whoever finds the world and becomes rich, let him renounce the world."

(111) Jesus said, "The heavens and the earth will be rolled up in your presence. And the one who lives from the living one will not see death." Does not Jesus say, "Whoever finds himself is superior to the world?"

(112) Jesus said, "Woe to the flesh that depends on the soul; woe to the soul that depends on the flesh."

(113) His disciples said to him, "When will the kingdom come?" Jesus said, "It will not come by waiting for it. It will not be a matter of saying 'here it is' or 'there it is.' Rather, the kingdom of the father is spread out upon the earth, and men do not see it."

(114) Simon Peter said to him, "Let Mary leave us, for women are not worthy of life." Jesus said, "I myself shall lead her in order to make her male, so that she too may

become a living spirit resembling you males. For every woman who will make herself male will enter the kingdom of heaven."

2 - The Didache

This document had been built in layers, the first six chapters apparently originated about 50 CE (20 years after the resurrection) and are credited to the second generation Christians, who are generally referred to as the Apostolic Fathers. Additional chapters were added as the church structure and theology were developed, the final form as set out below is thought to be representative of the early church's position in the mid to late second century.

There are several sections of the Didache that illustrates this 'add-on the layers' approach very nicely. Chapter 7 deals with baptism and it uses the words Father, Son and Holy Spirit, but this idea of the holy Trinity was not being seriously discussed until about the time Matthew was writing his Gospel in 80 CE, 50 years after the crucifixion. Chapter 8 amends the prayer Jesus gave his followers by asserting that God is in heaven, which exists somewhere other than on earth. These additions are evident in the Gospel of Matthew, an indication that the fundamental understanding of the very early Christians began to evolve and change very quickly.

Chapters 1 to 6 of the Didache summarize very nicely the teachings of Jesus as discussed in the first chapter of this book, and were well developed by 50 CE. Didache chapters 7 to 16 deal with operational issues that standardize ritual and liturgy across the movement. They are not reflective of the teachings of Jesus, they are the creation of men.

The Didache - The Lord's Teaching Through the Twelve Apostles to the Nations.

Chapter 1. The Two Ways and the first Commandment. There are two ways, one of life and one of death, but a great difference between the two ways. The way of life, then, is this: first, you shall love God who made you; second, love your neighbour as yourself, and do not do to another what you would not want done to you. And of these sayings the teaching is this: Bless those who curse you, and pray for your enemies, and fast for those who persecute you. For what reward is there for loving those who love you? Do not the Gentiles do the same? But love those who hate you, and you shall not have an enemy. Abstain from fleshly and worldly lusts. If someone strikes your right cheek, turn to him the other also, and you shall be perfect. If someone impresses you for one mile, go with him two. If someone takes your cloak, give him also your coat. If someone takes from you what is yours, ask it not back, for indeed you are not able. Give to everyone who asks you, and ask it not back; for the Father wills that to all should be given of our own blessings (free gifts). Happy is he who gives according to the commandment, for he is guiltless. Woe to him who receives; for if one receives who has need, he is guiltless; but he who receives not having need shall pay the penalty, why he received and for what. And coming into confinement, he shall be examined concerning the things which he has done, and he shall not escape from there until he pays back the last penny. And also concerning this, it has been said, let your alms sweat in your hands, until you know to whom you should give.

Chapter 2. The Second Commandment: Grave Sin Forbidden. And the second commandment of the Teaching; You shall not commit murder, you shall not commit adultery, you shall not commit pederasty, you shall not commit fornication, you shall not steal, you shall not practice magic, you shall not practice witchcraft, you shall not murder a child by abortion nor kill that which is born. You shall not covet the things of your neighbour, you shall not swear, you shall not bear false witness, you shall not speak evil, you shall bear no grudge. You shall not be double-minded nor double-tongued, for to be double-tongued is a snare of death. Your speech shall not be false, nor empty, but fulfilled by deed. You shall not be covetous, nor rapacious, nor a hypocrite, nor evil disposed, nor haughty. You shall not take evil counsel against your neighbour. You shall not hate any man; but some you shall reprove, and concerning some you shall pray, and some you shall love more than your own life.

Chapter 3. Other Sins Forbidden. My child, flee from every evil thing, and from every likeness of it. Be not prone to anger, for anger leads to murder. Be neither jealous, nor quarrelsome, nor of hot temper, for out of all these murders are engendered. My child, be not a lustful one. For lust leads to fornication. Be neither a filthy talker, nor of lofty eye, for out of all these adulteries are engendered. My child, be not an observer of omens, since it leads to idolatry. Be neither an enchanter, nor an astrologer, nor a purifier, nor be willing to look at these things, for out of all these idolatry is engendered. My child, be not a liar, since a lie leads to theft. Be neither money-loving, nor vainglorious, for out of all these thefts are engendered. My child, be not a murmurer, since it leads the way to blasphemy. Be neither self-willed nor evil-minded, for out of all these blasphemies are engendered.

Rather, be meek, since the meek shall inherit the earth. Be long-suffering and pitiful and guileless and gentle and good and always trembling at the words which you have heard. You shall not exalt yourself, nor give over-confidence to your soul. Your soul shall not be joined with lofty ones, but with just and lowly ones shall it have its intercourse. Accept whatever happens to you as good, knowing that apart from God nothing comes to pass.

Chapter 4. Various Precepts. My child, remember night and day him who speaks the word of God to you, and honour him as you do the Lord. For wherever the lordly rule is uttered, there is the Lord. And seek out day by day the faces of the saints, in order that you may rest upon their words. Do not long for division, but rather bring those who contend to peace. Judge righteously, and do not respect persons in reproving for transgressions. You shall not be undecided whether or not it shall be. Be not a stretcher forth of the hands to receive and a drawer of them back to give. If you have anything, through your hands you shall give ransom for your sins. Do not hesitate to give, nor complain when you give; for you shall know who is the good repayer of the hire. Do not turn away from him who is in want; rather, share all things with your brother, and do not say that they are your own. For if you are partakers in that which is immortal, how much more in things which are mortal? Do not remove your hand from your son or daughter; rather, teach them the fear of God from their youth. Do not enjoin anything in your bitterness upon your bondman or maidservant, who hope in the same God, lest ever they shall fear not God who is over both; for he comes not to call according to the outward appearance, but to them whom the Spirit has prepared. And you bondmen shall be subject to your masters as to a type of God, in modesty and fear. You shall hate all hypocrisy and everything which is not pleasing to the Lord. Do not in any way forsake the commandments of the Lord; but keep what you have received, neither adding thereto nor taking away therefrom. In the church you shall acknowledge your transgressions, and you shall not come near for your prayer with an evil conscience. This is the way of life.

Chapter 5. The Way of Death. And the way of death is this: first of all it is evil and accursed: murders, adultery, lust, fornication, thefts, idolatries, magic arts, witchcrafts, rape, false witness, hypocrisy, double-heartedness, deceit, haughtiness, depravity, self-will, greediness, filthy talking, jealousy, over-confidence, loftiness, boastfulness; persecutors of the good, hating truth, loving a lie, not knowing a reward for righteousness, not cleaving to good nor to righteous judgment, watching not for that which is good, but for that which is evil; from whom meekness and endurance are far, loving vanities, pursuing revenge, not pitying a poor man, not labouring for the afflicted, not knowing Him Who made them, murderers of children, destroyers of the handiwork of God, turning away from him who is in want, afflicting him who is distressed, advocates of the rich, lawless judges of the poor, utter sinners. Be delivered, children, from all these.

Chapter 6. Against False Teachers, and Food Offered to Idols. See that no one causes you to err from this way of the Teaching, since apart from God it teaches you. For if you are able to bear the entire yoke of the Lord, you will be perfect; but if you are not able to do this, do what you are able. And concerning food, bear what you are able; but against that which is sacrificed to idols be exceedingly careful; for it is the service of dead gods.

Chapter 7. Concerning Baptism. And concerning baptism, baptize this way: Having first said all these things, baptize into the name of the Father, and of the Son, and of the Holy Spirit, in living water. But if you have no living water, baptize into other water; and if you cannot do so in cold water, do so in warm. But if you have neither, pour out water three times upon the head into the name of Father and Son and Holy Spirit. But before the baptism let the baptizer fast, and the baptized, and whoever else can; but you shall order the baptized to fast one or two days before.

Chapter 8. Fasting and Prayer (the Lord's Prayer). But let not your fasts be with the hypocrites, for they fast on the second and fifth day of the week. Rather, fast on the fourth day and the Preparation (Friday). Do not pray like the hypocrites, but rather as the Lord commanded in His , like this:

Our Father who is in heaven, hallowed be Your name. Your kingdom come. Your will be done on earth, as it is in heaven. Give us today our daily (needful) bread, and forgive us our debt as we also forgive our debtors. And bring us not into temptation, but deliver us from the evil one (or, evil); for Yours is the power and the glory for ever...

Pray this three times each day.

Chapter 9. The Eucharist. Now concerning the Eucharist, give thanks this way. first, concerning the cup:

We thank You, our Father, for the holy vine of David Your servant, which You made known to us through Jesus Your Servant; to You be the glory for ever...

And concerning the broken bread:

We thank You, our Father, for the life and knowledge which You madest known to us through Jesus Your Servant; to You be the glory for ever. Even as this broken bread was scattered over the hills, and was gathered together and became one, so let your Church be gathered together from the ends of the earth into Your kingdom; for Yours is the glory and the power through Jesus Christ for ever.

But let no one eat or drink of your Eucharist, unless they have been baptized into the name of the Lord; for concerning this also the Lord has said, "Give not that which is holy to the dogs."

Chapter 10. Prayer after Communion. But after you are filled, give thanks this way:

We thank You, Holy Father, for Your holy name which You placed in our hearts, and for the knowledge and faith and immortality, which You made known to us through Jesus Your Servant; to You be the glory for ever. You, Master almighty, created all things for Your name's sake; You gave food and drink to men for enjoyment, that they might give thanks to You; but to us You freely gave spiritual food and drink and life eternal through Your Servant. Before all things we thank You that You are mighty; to You be the glory for ever. Remember, Lord, Your Church, to deliver it from all evil and to make it perfect in Your love, and gather it from the four winds, sanctified for Your kingdom which You have prepared for it; for Yours is the power and the glory for ever. Let grace come, and let this world pass away. Hosanna to the God (Son) of David! If anyone is holy, let him come; if anyone is not so, let him repent. Maranatha. Amen.

But permit the prophets to make Thanksgiving as much as they desire.

Chapter 11. Concerning Teachers, Apostles, and Prophets. Whosoever, therefore, comes and teaches you all these things that have been said before, receive him. But if the teacher himself turns and teaches another doctrine to the destruction of this, hear him not. But if he teaches so as to increase righteousness and the knowledge of the Lord, receive him as the Lord. But concerning the apostles and prophets, act according to the decree of the . Let every apostle who comes to you be received as the Lord. But he shall not remain more than one day; or two days, if there's a need. But if he remains three days, he is a false prophet. And when the apostle goes away, let him take nothing but bread until he lodges. If he asks for money, he is a false prophet. And every prophet who speaks in the Spirit you shall neither try nor judge; for every sin shall be forgiven, but this sin shall not be forgiven. But not everyone who speaks in the Spirit is a prophet; but only if he holds the ways of the Lord. Therefore, from their ways shall the false prophet and the prophet be known. And every prophet who orders a meal in the Spirit does not eat it, unless he is indeed a false prophet. And every prophet who teaches the truth, but does not do what he teaches, is a false prophet. And every prophet, proved true, working unto the mystery of the Church in the world, yet not teaching others to do what he himself does, shall not be judged among you, for with God he has his judgment; for so did also the ancient prophets. But whoever says in the Spirit, Give me money, or something else, you shall not listen to him. But if he tells you to give for others' sake who are in need, let no one judge him.

Chapter 12. Reception of Christians. But receive everyone who comes in the name of the Lord, and prove and know him afterward; for you shall have understanding right and left. If he who comes is a wayfarer, assist him as far as you are able; but he shall not remain with you more than two or three days, if need be. But if he wants to stay with you, and is an artisan, let him work and eat. But if he has no trade, according to your understanding, see to it that, as a Christian, he shall not live with you idle. But if he wills not to do, he is a Christ-monger. Watch that you keep away from such.

Chapter 13. Support of Prophets. But every true prophet who wants to live among you is worthy of his support. So also a true teacher is himself worthy, as the workman, of his support. Every first-fruit, therefore, of the products of wine-press and threshing-floor, of oxen and of sheep, you shall take and give to the prophets, for they are your high priests. But if you have no prophet, give it to the poor. If you make a batch of dough, take the first-fruit and give according to the commandment. So also when you open a jar of wine or of oil, take the first-fruit and give it to the prophets; and of money (silver) and clothing and every possession, take the first-fruit, as it may seem good to you, and give according to the commandment.

Chapter 14. Christian Assembly on the Lord's Day. But every Lord's day gather yourselves together, and break bread, and give thanksgiving after having confessed your transgressions, that your sacrifice may be pure. But let no one who is at odds with his fellow come together with you, until they be reconciled, that your sacrifice may not be profaned. For this is that which was spoken by the Lord: "In every place and time offer to me a pure sacrifice; for I am a great King, says the Lord, and my name is wonderful among the nations."

Chapter 15. Bishops and Deacons; Christian Reproof. Appoint, therefore, for yourselves, bishops and deacons worthy of the Lord, men meek, and not lovers of money, and truthful and proved; for they also render to you the service of prophets and teachers. Therefore do not despise them, for they are your honoured ones, together with the prophets and teachers. And reprove one another, not in anger, but in peace, as you have it in the . But to anyone that acts amiss against another, let no one speak, nor let him hear anything from you until he repents. But your prayers and alms and all your deeds so do, as you have it in the of our Lord.

Chapter 16. Watchfulness; the Coming of the Lord. Watch for your life's sake. Let not your lamps be quenched, nor your loins unloosed; but be ready, for you know not the hour in which our Lord will come. But come together often, seeking the things which are befitting to your souls: for the whole time of your faith will not profit you, if you are not made perfect in the last time. For in the last days false prophets and corrupters shall be multiplied, and the sheep shall be turned into wolves, and love shall be turned into hate; for when lawlessness increases, they shall hate and persecute and betray one another, and then shall appear the world-deceiver as Son of God, and shall do signs and wonders, and the earth shall be delivered into his hands, and he shall do iniquitous things which have never yet come to pass since the beginning. Then shall the creation of men come into the fire of trial, and many shall be made to stumble and shall perish; but those who endure in their faith shall be saved from under the curse itself. And then shall appear the signs of the truth: first, the sign of an outspreading in heaven, then the sign of the sound of the trumpet. And third, the resurrection of the dead -- yet not of all, but as it is said: "The Lord shall come and all His saints with Him." Then shall the world see the Lord coming upon the clouds of heaven.

3 - Bibliography

This investigative journey began when I was a teenager over 50 years ago, and I have been reading everything I could find through these many years. Building a career and raising a family while coping with significant health challenges resulted in this being a part time endeavour, and I had no idea where it would lead until I got there, I was truly surprised at the outcome.

It is impossible for me to list all of the sources that contributed to my research, one can safely say that virtually anything that was written on the subject in the 20th century was fair game and might very well have influenced me. And of course in the 21st century we have the Internet, a resource that I used frequently. A resource that required considerable care however, because information presented there is not necessarily grounded in solid research or facts; wherever I relied on information from this public and very democratic domain the information was substantiated by at least one other reliable source. When I approached the task in earnest with a view to documenting my journey I did rely on the following books and websites as reference points.

The New Testament
Steven L. Davies, 2011
ISBN 978-1-59815-036-0
Polebridge Press
Willamette University, 900 State Street,
Salem, OR 97301

The Other Jesus
Greg Garrett, 2011
ISBN 978-0-664-23404-1
Westminster John Knox Press
100 Witherspoon Street, Louisville,
Kentucky 40202-1396

With or Without God
Gretta Vosper, 2008
ISBN 978-1-55468-228-7
HarperCollins Publishers Ltd
2 Bloor Street East, 20th Floor, Toronto,
Ontario, Canada, M4W IA8

The Lost History of Christianity
Philip Jenkins, 2008
ISBN 978 -0-06-147280-0
HarperCollins Publishers
10 East 53rd Street, New York, NY 10022

Lost Scripture
Bart D. Ehrman, 2003
ISBN 0-19-514182-2
Oxford University Press

198 Madison Avenue, New York 10016

Whose Bible Is It?
Jaroslav Pelikan, 2005
ISBN 0-670-03385-5
Penguin Books Ltd
80 Strand, London WC2R 0RL, England

The Five s
Robert W. Funk, Roy W. Hoover, and the
Jesus Seminar, 1993
ISBN 978-0-06-063040-9
HarperCollins Publishers
10 East 53rd Street, New York, NY 10022

Killing Jesus
Bill O'Reilly, Martin Dugard, 2013
ISBN 978-0-8050-9854-9
Henry Holt and Company, LLC
175 Fifth Avenue New York, New York
10010

The Faith Instinct
Nicholas Wade, 2009
ISBN 978-1-59420-228-5
Penguin Books Ltd
80 Strand, London WC2R 0RL, England

www.earlychristianwriting.com
www.xenos.org
www.jewishhistory.org

www.ingramcontent.com/pod-product-compliance
Lightning Source LLC
LaVergne TN
LVHW051458080426
835509LV00017B/1807